Rebirth of the Oracle

The Tarot for the Modern World

by

Justine A. Alessi
M. E. McMillan

OZARK
MOUNTAIN
PUBLISHING

P.O. Box 754
Huntsville, AR 72740

For permission, or serialization, condensation, adaptions, or for catalog of other publications, write to: Ozark Mountain publishing, Inc., P.O. Box 754, Huntsville, AR 72740, Attn: Permissions Department.

Library of Congress Cataloging-in-Publication Data
Alessi, Justine A. - 1949 -
McMilla, M. E. - 1952 -
"Rebirth of the Oracle" by Justine A. Alessi and M.E. McMillan
Modern interpretations for the ancient symbols of the Tarot cards.

1. Tarot   2. Divination   3. Games

I. Alessi, Justine, 1949 - II. McMillian, M.E., 1952 - III. Title IV. Tarot
Library of Congress Catalog Card Number: 2005922108
ISBN: 1-886940-89-4

Cover Art and Layout by Victoria Cooper Art
Book Design: Julia Degan
Book Set in: Times New Roman

Published By

P.O. Box 754, Huntsville, AR 72740
www.ozarkmt.com
Printed in the United States of
America

This book is dedicated to Queens of Cups everywhere.

Acknowledgements

I would like to thank my wonderful husband, Bob, for thirty five years of loving support for whatever I choose to do, including writing this book. The experiences of being a wife, mother, daughter, sister, grandmother and friend have provided a fountain of wisdom for me to draw on when I help other people seek enlightenment using the Tarot. I would have an incredible list of names if I were to thank everyone who has helped me accomplish this. Therefore, I will broadly and gratefully thank everyone who has given me the privilege of "reading their cards." I also offer love and gratitude to my daughter, Marianne Foderetti and her husband, Joe, my son, Anthony, my beautiful granddaughter, Maryelise and my grandsons, Jason, Peter, Nicholas and Patrick, who always believed that someday this book would be written. My family has also been very excited watching the progress of this book. They include my mother, Justine Masi my sisters, Jean Weis, Janet Mascaro and Joann Conwell and their families. I would also like to recognize the amazing encouragement from my friends, Selene Bean, Jenny Howes, Judy Pugliese, Trudy Hudson and Amy Dunn.

I have loved many people who have gone to the next lifetime and I know they are my angels. I remember my father, Anthony Masi, my mother in law, Inez Alessi and my dear friends, Jean Stasko, Ada Page, Eileen Morrison and Brenda Philip. They were all looking over my shoulder while every word of this book was written.

Justine Alessi

I would like to thank my husband, Jim, my son, Chris, my daughter, Meredith, my mother, Nancy Boyle and my father, the late Joseph Boyle Sr. for their many years of patience and understanding in the evolution of my writing career. And I would also like to acknowledge my very dear friends, the late Mike Johnson, Anna Belle Faile, Forest and Vicki Ratliff, Bonnie Misch, Albert Dispenza, J. P. Giles, Steve Kersten, Joe Buckley, Elizabeth Lytle-Wilcox and Steve Zachar for their unswerving support and encouragement.

M. E. (Betsy) McMillan

And we offer our most sincere thanks to Dolores Cannon, whose wisdom and vision made this dream a reality, and to Nancy Garrison and editor Julia Degan, members of her dedicated staff. Our thanks also to photographer Tony Phung for the wonderful portrait shots.

Special thanks to Tarot students extraordinaire, Donna Rudnay, Amber Devor, Dawn Steiner, and Sherry Jackson for participating in the process and for their insightful input.

Justine and Betsy
January 19, 2005

AUTHORS' NOTES

Rebirth of the Oracle; The Tarot for the Modern World is a book I thought about writing for over a decade. I first became interested in the Tarot in 1986, when I was given a deck of Tarot cards as a gift. I was fascinated by them, but confused. I wasn't quite sure what to do with them. There were relatively few books on the market at the time, but I purchased, read and attempted to make sense of what was available. It was a great struggle to glean the necessary knowledge from those books.

My first real understanding of the Tarot came under the tutelage of a friend, Cheryl Molina-Grey. Cheryl was from Tucson, AZ and knew a great deal about the Tarot. She recommended that I read "The Tarot of the Bohemians". I worked hard to understand it, but only after a few one-on-one sessions with Cheryl did I begin to easily grasp the concepts. I learned that Tarot cards are an oracle, and oracles have a way of making themselves clear.

One thing she taught me is that, if given the basics of the Tarot, most people interpreting the cards will arrive at the same conclusions as to their meanings. Unfortunately, not everyone who wishes to read the cards has a Cheryl Grey for a mentor! Cheryl passed away several years ago at a relatively young age, but I will certainly never forget her ease with the Tarot and all that she taught me.

Over the next years, I found that I not only understood the cards, but they spoke very clearly to me. What started out as a hobby became my passion! In 1989, I retired from my job as a librarian and immersed myself in the study and interpretation of the cards. I found in them a uniqueness that has never been equaled in my life. Reading the Tarot is the most enlightening, enjoyable and gratifying phenomenon I have ever experienced.

Most of the Tarot books on the shelves today are confusing and difficult to understand. I hear frequent complaints from others that wading through the esoteric language and the various authors' interpretations of the symbolism has discouraged them from learning about the cards. When I taught the same people in my Tarot classes, I inevitably was approached with comments such as, "You made understanding the cards so simple. Why don't YOU write a book that people can understand?" *Rebirth of the Oracle* is my response to those requests.

I believe that the Tarot is for everyone, and although it is an ancient oracle dating from the twelfth century, the Tarot holds as much illumination, consolation and validation for the twenty-first century as it did in the twelfth. My aspiration became to write a book that everyone could understand and to demystify the cards. In this millennium, when the world is in turmoil and people crave spirituality and answers, the Tarot has again found its place.

Enlisting the aid of my dear friend and fellow Queen of Cups, Betsy McMillan, a writer with a magical way of bringing words to life, we embarked on the creation of this book. Betsy and I wrote and rewrote. We taught classes to learn what people wanted to know and received valued input from other Tarot enthusiasts. We even commissioned a marketing survey (conducted by Gemini Development Group of Solon, Ohio) to determine the best format for this book. The survey concluded that the public wanted a concise, easy-to-read book, and that bullet-point definitions were the prevalent choice of a cross section of people across the United States.

As a culmination of all those efforts and years of Tarot experience, we offer you *Rebirth of the Oracle: The Tarot for the Modern World* as our contribution to easily understanding and interpreting the cards with significant application to the twenty-first century.

Justine Alessi, June, 2003

When I first met Justine a little over 12 years ago, I was just another curious person who wanted a reading. A co-worker had recommended I give Justine a chance to impress me with her accuracy. I walked in, shook her hand, and knew immediately that a long-term friendship had just been kindled. But that was the icing on the cake. She read my cards with an attention to detail and an accuracy factor I did not believe possible. I was also struck by the fact that Justine seemed "normal" when compared to other readers I had encountered over the years. No neon palm in the window, no outlandish garb, no crystal ball; there was nothing at all about Justine that was designed to overwhelm the lay person with mystery and mysticism. There was no drama, she just told it as she saw it in the cards.

My interest in the Tarot grew, as did our friendship. Needless to say, when Justine approached me to co-author a book on Tarot, I was both flattered and challenged. I put aside several fiction projects, and we set about the task of writing a book that would be as straightforward and as easy to understand as Justine was when giving a reading. The seemingly endless task was really a labor of love. Countless e-mails, rewrites, Tarot classes, procrastination (we are Queens of Cups!), and even more rewrites have dominated this three-year gestation period. I am happy (and relieved!) to announce that the baby has finally arrived. Christened *Rebirth of the Oracle: The Tarot for the Modern World*, a book couldn't have two prouder parents. We hope that your journey in learning about the Tarot will be a better and more satisfying one with *Rebirth of the Oracle* at your side.

M. E. "Betsy" McMillan, June 2003

CONTENTS

INTRODUCTION

Welcome to the incredibly beautiful and intriguing world of the Tarot. The purpose of this book, *Rebirth of the Oracle - The Tarot for the Modern World*, is to simplify and demystify this ancient oracle and to make it accessible to anyone who would like to read the cards.

The meanings given to the cards in this book are drawn from the experiences of thousands of readings. They are also written with an eye toward updating the Tarot, bringing this ancient oracle into the 21st century. You will see meanings displayed for the cards that were not heard of, or even dreamed of, in the early centuries of the Tarot. These include everything from media exposure to abortion to identity theft.

There are no right or wrong meanings to the cards. Interestingly, even if an intuitive reader has never studied a book, he or she will ultimately draw the same or similar conclusions as other readers. Remember, the Tarot is an oracle, and the oracle speaks to the reader.

Tarot reading can be a very insightful tool, and many questions go much deeper than the present situation. There is no preferred method of reading the Tarot. The reader is at liberty to combine her intuition, her psychic third eye and all the information she has acquired regarding the Tarot to arrive at the appropriate conclusions.

When you read the Tarot, all that matters is what the cards say to YOU. Let the thoughts flow as you look at the cards. Keep in mind, that as an oracle, they will make themselves clear to you. Handle the cards often. Note how they "feel" when you lay out a spread. Ask friends to be your guinea pigs. They will get a kick out of it, and you will gain much needed experience and the opportunity to hone your delivery. When you begin to dream the cards, then you are really ready to read them for others.

Tarot reading is pure pleasure and gratification to me. Knowing that you can ease a broken heart or give hope or show that there is a light at the end of the tunnel is what makes the Tarot so fulfilling and fascinating! Just do your best. Know your cards and rely on your intuition for the rest. It will come very easily to you the more you practice.

Many centuries ago, the Tarot was only to be consulted by Egyptian priests and priestesses. Now, it's available to all of us. What a wonderful thing that is! I hope all of you reading this book will grow to love the Tarot as much as I do!

Justine

Section 1:

THE COURT CARDS

...And in the grand scheme of things, the Creator said, "Instill these creatures, made in my image, with some small part of me to keep this world I have created in balance." And so the Cup people were endowed with the Heart of God, the Pentacle people with the intellect of God, the Sword people with the Power of God and the Wand people with the Hands of God. And the Creator said, "It is good."

INTRODUCTION TO THE COURT CARDS

For the experienced Tarot reader, it is relatively simple to use one's intuitive ability to choose a significator card. As a reader, one develops the gift of discerning the energy flowing from another person. In-depth knowledge of the characteristics of the other Court Cards that may appear in the reading makes interpretation much more accurate and specific. For the new reader, or for a person who wishes to understand her own signification, or the signification of people that her reader predicts will come into and influence her life, understanding the characteristics of the court cards is essential. Whether an experienced reader, a novice or a lay person, the information in this book is invaluable.

Much like the definitive explanation of the Zodiac Signs, Rebirth of the Oracle provides the reader with a very informative view of each of the court cards and a detailed explanation of the personality, drives and nuances of each person. In reading Court Cards, generally the upright position indicates positive personality traits and the reversed position indicates the more negative aspects, or that the influence of that particular person will not be particularly impactful.

Most people are one signification type and remain so all of their adult lives. However, there will occasionally be such a momentous change in one's life or attitude that it is indeed possible to cross over into another type of personality. This takes an extraordinary amount of will. Also, albeit infrequently, there exist individuals who seem to be a blend of two personalities. If qualities of two court cards are observed in a single individual, I recommend focusing on the court card that represents the greater percentage of his or her applicable qualities.

As a general rule, Kings are men in their maturity, and whether they are 25 or 65, the perception of a King is that of a man who is truly comfortable with himself. Most men will be significated as Knights from approximately 19 to 25, but again, there are men up to age 50 and older who never really mature and continue to exhibit Knight qualities.

All women past eighteen are Queens. The younger children, and even the teenagers of the Tarot, will be significated as pages. You may notice that a page description will say either "he" or "she" throughout the profile. This is simply written for flow, and a page can be male or female (page or princess if you prefer), regardless of suit.

It does not necessarily follow, for example, that all Pages of Cups will grow up to be Queens of Cups or that all Knights of Wands will grow to be Kings of Wands. As with all things in life, the mature personality is formed by family and environment; therefore, the mature adult is often far removed from his or her teenaged self.

The more understanding the reader has of the characteristics of the Court Cards, the better, more informative and more accurate the reading will be. As a Tarot reader, I find that the more detail I can offer, the more enlightening the reading becomes, and the person for whom I am reading finds the information specific and helpful. We offer here these extensively researched characteristics and methods of signification, based on years of reading experience. All the material contained in this book is gleaned from my own reading history. Keep in mind, when reading the cards, that what the cards say to YOU is the answer you seek.

THE KING OF CUPS

KING of CUPS.

THE BASICS:

- ♥ Also known as: The King of Hearts
- ♥ Sign: Chameleon
- ♥ Flower: Amaryllis
- ♥ Gemstone: Ruby
- ♥ Characteristics: Self-reliant, emotionally distant, ambivalent
- ♥ Best Relationships: Queen of Swords, King of Wands, Queen of Wands
- ♥ Watchwords: "I would like to try that with you...but please don't come too close."
- ♥ Manifestations of the spirit world: Dreams, visions, scents, voices of the deceased

GENERAL

As fascinating and unfathomable as a prism, the King of Cups shows a different facet of his personality, as appropriate, for each occasion, or depending on the company at a particular moment. The King of Hearts in a regular deck comes across, at a minimum, as both heads and tails of the same coin with all the vast differences that contrast implies.

The man you get is totally dependent on who you are. Some are lucky enough to bring out his best (but generally hidden) attributes, while the rest of the population might describe him as cold, impersonal, uninterested, perhaps even totally unavailable emotionally. Although he may appear that way to most people, underneath that staid and almost unfriendly exterior is a highly emotional and sensitive human being.

Likely a victim of a traumatically broken relationship, he learned early on to keep his emotional side in check. This early trauma could have been the sudden loss of a best friend, sibling, parent or significant other. He may have been the victim of a childhood illness, in some way set apart from other kids or a victim of peer teasing. He keeps a good distance away from others emotionally to minimize the likelihood of enduring more hurt. If by some stroke of luck you are privileged to gain access to the man behind the facade, you will be rewarded with honesty, sincerity and faithfulness. The "real" King of Cups has a truly good heart.

The King of Cups is a dreamer. He has an ideal of life (what it should be like, who he should be with) so firmly entrenched in his mind that he finds it difficult to find contentment in the hand he is dealt.

His highly psychic abilities rival those of the Queen of Cups, but about 90% of these Kings bury that ability. It is yet another attempt to minimize the possibility of causing himself more involvement and more emotional pain. In spite of not using this talent, the King is a wonderful listener, able to relate well to others, and he is excellent in the role of advisor or counselor.

5

PERSONALITY

The King is not just attentive to detail; he is meticulous about the fine points. If he is a reader, he can find flaws or inconsistencies in any book. He remembers in such detail that he can spot inconsistencies not only within a particular volume, but also from one book to the next in a series. He is endlessly fascinated by new technology and likely owns the latest and greatest techno-gadgets. He is up-to-date on cutting-edge technological developments, especially in electronics and computer hardware and peripherals. If he finds a new product interesting, he won't hesitate to try it, and then purchase one.

Once he owns something, the King will care for it, keeping it clean and properly stored when not in use. He is not careless with his possessions; he works too hard for them. But he doesn't buy things rashly. He buys only what he really wants and does not lend his possessions out or give them away easily. By the same token, he doesn't ask to borrow from others either, living by the old adage "Neither a borrower nor a lender be." Occasionally you will run across an aberrant King of Cups who goes to the other end of the spectrum, with lavish spending and gift-giving habits. Unfortunately, this spending King often attaches emotional baggage to the gifts he gives: love, expectation, hope, anticipation, longing.

He is not afraid to try something new, at least not technologically speaking. When it comes to food, forget dragging him to that new Mongolian restaurant. He knows what he likes, and he will stubbornly refuse to try anything that might taste differently. He has his limits. Don't try to compete with his mother in the cooking department; no one can make apple pie as good as his mom's! And he will never cease reminding you of that fact.

Although the King will travel on occasion, he is most happy when he is at home. If he does travel, he plans for it meticulously, researching the destination to be sure it is a place he might like, comparing prices to get the best rates. It may be for fun, but there's no point in paying more than necessary. And although he takes the time to research, he often ends up not finalizing the plan until the last minute, just in case some better rate comes up in the meantime. Generally, he would rather be at home watching a favorite show or playing with his computer or newest techno-toy.

The King is an introspective person and a deep thinker. He has at least one place where he can sit and contemplate the issues that are bothering him, or to indulge in active daydreaming. It could be a favorite room, a cubbyhole in the basement, or some special place in the woods with his name on it, but it is most definitely someplace where he feels comfortable and can find solitude.

He may have been spoiled a bit as a child and was likely the youngest in the family. He may even get angry and act out if he doesn't get to have things his way, especially if the issue is important to him. However, as in all the King's relationship issues, how he reacts depends enormously on the person he is with at the time of the upset and how far he can push that person without pushing him or her away. He knows how far he can go, and when to back off in an anger situation. However, he is not known for his tact or diplomacy.

He loves his mother deeply and will do anything for her. He is often the child that ends up taking care of his parents as they age. He has an uncommon respect and softness toward his elders, and deals with them in a very calm, gentle and understanding manner. His ability to quietly listen comes in very handy when dealing with the older folks, as they often ply him with war stories and old memories of their lives, and he endures the telling and retelling of those tales with the patience of Job.

Often described as the lone-wolf type, the King of Cups sometimes stays single for life. He is more than capable of surviving on his own, but if he does take a mate, he will work hard to provide and to make the relationship work. He is not the type to keep the little woman barefoot and pregnant. He encourages his mate to pursue a career and to have her own interests. He finds their differences appealing and intellectually stimulating. In the same vein, he encourages his children to finish their schooling, get jobs at young ages and leave the nest as early as possible, as long as they are capable of flight.

Like a chameleon blending into the background, the King of Cups is forever absorbing everything around him. He is a keen observer of life. He remains quiet and just sits back and takes in what others are saying. It is not that he has nothing to say himself, but just as he does with money, he gathers information in and saves it up just in case he needs to use it later. He actively seeks information on topics that interest him, and when he studies something, he is very single-minded in the pursuit of that knowledge until his thirst for information on the subject is quenched.

When he does speak up, pouring forth an abundance of knowledge on a given topic, people are always surprised. He is so quiet they never suspect that he's harboring such a wealth of information. If he has a partner, he will confide his thoughts in her (or him), because he's dependent on his mate for emotional support. Any insecurities the King keeps hidden are usually dealt with by the application of the loving confidence of his mate.

The King of Cups does exceedingly well at trivia games and brainteasers. He could sit and watch kids and animals play for hours, and he is always amazed at the intelligence he sees in them that others never notice.

EMPLOYMENT

As mentioned before, the King of Cups has an incredible capacity for detail. He is generally very good at any job that relies on mathematics or industrial theory. He makes an excellent mechanic, if that is his interest. He is also a whiz on anything new or high tech. If he is a compu-phile, he loves and cares for his computer and can fix any hardware or software problem. He is often found working the "help desk" or may be a LAN or network administrator.

He is interested in books and reading (subjects he likes of course) and his attention to detail may land him a job as an editor or proofreader. He wishes he could write, and quite likely he could if he set his mind to the task, but he is content reading the work of other authors.

His ability to remain detached while listening attentively makes the King of Cups very adept at positions that involve counseling; e.g., social worker, cleric, psychologist, etc. And although he will not readily admit it, his very active imagination and ability to role-play make him an accomplished actor, should he choose the stage as his avocation.

APPEARANCE

The King of Cups makes a good poker player. He not only plays cards well, but his emotions don't show readily on his face. It is easy for him to conceal his thoughts, even from those who know him well. When particularly self-absorbed he appears somewhat glassy-eyed and very far away from the here and now.

After a hard day at work, he would rather come home and relax than gear up for a lot of recreational or necessary (as in yard work) physical activity. As a result, he sometimes struggles with his weight. But his physique and condition are generally such that if he works out, even a little, he improves quickly. The King is very aware of his "jiggles" when he has them, and he will do something about them eventually.

He buys quality clothing, but is far from being a clotheshorse. He has his favorites and tends to keep wearing them again and again because he looks good and feels comfortable in them. He can be a bit vain; he cares about his appearance and works to enhance his good features. The King almost always grows old gracefully, which is not too much of a chore since the raw material he started with was much better than most. In fact, he tends to be very attractive, regardless of his age or stage in life.

MONEY

Frugal is an inept description for the King of Cups. Some would call him a skinflint, but he knows himself best, and he will semi-seriously call himself a "scrooge." He works hard for everything he has, and what he has earned is his exclusively. He is reticent to waste money or to give it away unnecessarily.

Unlike many of us, he is always looking for a genuine bargain. The King relentlessly (and intelligently) pays off the balances on his credit cards every month. It is against his personal beliefs to pay interest charges unless there is an emergency situation. He shops on-line, eats at the local family restaurant or pub, and he is not so stingy that he won't offer to pay for your dinner. But he is loath to pay $100 for macaroni and cheese for two at some grossly over-priced gourmet bistro.

He always has money for a rainy day or an emergency, and he will always have sufficient retirement funds socked away. So you see, his penny pinching will pay off in the end because he is always saving money--just in case.

EMOTIONS

The King of Cups never seems totally happy. He has big dreams and exceptionally high expectations, and is always waiting for something special to happen; e.g., meeting the perfect woman, getting the perfect job, winning the lottery. Even while he is wishing for the ultimate, he fears that he will never attain those perfect things he believes will finally make him happy.

He has difficulty appreciating what is offered to him freely. He overanalyzes in an effort to find out what may not be "perfect" about it, or simply because he won't consider accepting that which he views as imperfect. This applies to people as well as things. As a result, he tends to miss emotional and relationship opportunities.

He is discriminating in his choice of friends, but he shares a wonderful rapport with those he has acquired over the years. He may go for weeks or even months without contacting you at all.

But don't worry, he is not angry with you. He is just respecting your space, and he genuinely worries that too frequent contact might annoy or bother you.

Spending time alone is not a big problem for the King of Cups. He is truly content in his own company. He tends to be a loner and isn't one to express his emotions openly, unless he is very angry. But in spite of the firm control he keeps over his emotions, he has a strong creative bent. People are often surprised at his undertakings, be it fine art, acting or web design. Beneath that sometimes-dark exterior is a somewhat stifled creative heart screaming for release.

Although it may not seem obvious at first, he does have a sense of humor, although somewhat dry by most standards. He has a razor-sharp wit and can be a little (or a lot) sarcastic and somewhat insulting. The King of Cups has limits to his tolerance of others, especially toward those who constantly demonstrate blatant stupidity, and his sarcastic comments are often pointed toward those he views in that way. He can be bigoted toward those he sees as different from himself, but as long as they refrain from openly doing things he considers stupid, he will keep comment to himself. His acerbic wit and wealth of sarcasm may be considered by some as borderline verbal abuse, but he would never agree with that assessment.

On the flip side of the coin, he can be absolutely charming and engaging in social situations if he can be persuaded to open up and participate, a challenge at best. He tends to act shy, but actually enjoys attention, especially that of women. Like many men, he succumbs to flattery easily; compliments feed his emotional needs. The King of Cups feels everything deeply, both emotionally and physically. This combination can lead some Kings to sexual promiscuity, but even the most philandering King will pull up the reigns when he finds his true mate, and he will become an incredibly faithful partner and lover.

LOVE

The King of Cups' faithfulness is a fundamental part of his innate sense of commitment. Once he finds a mate, a friend or has a child, he works tirelessly to make the relationship with that person work. In the case of his life partner, he often tries to the point of co-dependency; doing and giving whatever is asked of him, even if the request is unreasonable.

He loves deeply and completely; so don't be fooled if he doesn't seem to express his feelings. Verbalizing is not his forte. Unfortunately, the combination of loving to the verge of co-dependency and the inability or unwillingness to verbalize his feelings can result in emotional turmoil and unintended clashes with his mate. They don't happen often, but they do happen.

The King of Cups often finds it difficult to give compliments. And when he likes someone, he worries that person might view him as fawning or suffering from "fan-boy" syndrome. Regardless of how close the relationship, don't be annoyed if the best compliment you get is, "You did okay." No matter whether he is only mildly impressed or absolutely astounded by what you do, you will generally get the same response.

He loves his children unconditionally. If he is childless, he will show incredible patience for the children of others such as nieces, nephews and the offspring of friends. He often goes out of his way to get some special items for others' kids if he is planning a visit. Usually the gifts will be some really nifty mechanical or technical gizmo; but then again, he is just buying what he knows he would have liked at their ages.

A fair percentage of Kings of Cups are gay or bisexual. They bring the same traits to those relationships that the straight King of Cups brings to his unions.

HEALTH

If there is some odd ailment out there for the taking, the King of Cups will find it and bring it home. Shingles, hives and skin rashes with no known cause are commonplace to the King. If the wind blows through poison ivy or oak, and he happens to be standing downwind, the blisters will soon follow.

Anything stress related is also a good bet for the King, including high blood pressure, twitches, ulcers and gastrointestinal problems. He often suffers from high cholesterol, and his particularly fussy eating habits tend to stifle his ability to take in a wide variety of healthy foods. Why should he eat those healthy things when steak and potatoes or greasy pizzas are readily available?

LEST WE FORGET

The King of Cups has a wellspring of self-knowledge and is generally content with the man that he is. If others misunderstand him, that is their problem. Regardless of his sexual proclivities, be prepared for a personality rife with dualism. He has a sensitive side, even when he is the most rugged and straight guy you can imagine. He likes certain types of art and music, including the classical stuff. He is fascinated by gadgets and loves to invent better mouse traps.

Living with him can be a roller-coaster ride; just remember that people pay good money for roller-coaster thrills--then sit back, take it in stride, and enjoy the King of Cups' ride.

THE QUEEN OF CUPS

QUEEN of CUPS.

THE BASICS:

- ♥ Also known as: The Queen of Hearts
- ♥ Sign: Butterfly
- ♥ Flower: Lilac
- ♥ Gemstone: Rose Quartz
- ♥ Characteristics: Tenacious, compassionate, psychic
- ♥ Best Relationships: King of Wands, Queen of Cups, Queen of Wands
- ♥ Watchwords: "I feel what you feel... I see what you cannot see".
- ♥ Manifestations of the spirit world: Dreams, visions, scents, voices of the deceased

GENERAL

It is with great delight and wonder that you welcome a butterfly that unexpectedly lands on or near you. You should greet the Queen of Cups in a similar way! Did you ever notice that she seems to show up out of the blue whenever you most need her? She stops just long enough to help; then she's gone like a butterfly on the breeze. No wonder that gentle and beautiful creature is the sign of the gracious and lovely Queen of Cups. There are those who say that such a butterfly is a deceased love one, staying near, watching out for you, or just saying hello. That makes a comparison with the Queen of Cups most appropriate.

She has attained her wisdom and status because she is a very old soul who has lived many lives, and, as an old soul, has interacted with the souls of many, most all of whom are many lifetimes younger. Perhaps she recognizes an old friend in you!

Taking care of those old friends, and the new ones, is a paramount concern for the Queen of Cups. Being the oldest of souls, she gives new meaning to "mother's instinct". As a matter of fact, she seems to have the art of mothering down to a science. Her home is her castle, and there she reigns supreme, but she rules with love. She spends her life caring for loved ones and worrying over those who have need of her wisdom and direction. But even as her home is her castle, her kingdom is without borders. You don't have to be her child, spouse, parent or sibling. She will hover over and care for any individual she believes could benefit from her motherly attentions. This pretty much includes the entire population of the kingdom, no matter how extensive that "kingdom" may be.

There is no such thing as a stranger in her world, and she often takes these "orphans" into her home as well as her life. As an old soul, she may just be seeing a friendly soul in a new and different body. Lifetimes of these "reacquainting herself with other souls" activities have made the Queen of Cups into a non-judgmental, positive, cheerful matriarch who accepts each person at face value; everyone has merit; everyone has redeeming qualities! She can clearly see the positive aspects of each person's personality, and does her best to cajole those aspects out into view.

Her obsession with bringing out the best in everyone often sees her taking odd "characters" under her tutelage. Benefiting from her nurturing direction, each ugly duckling becomes a swan, each Eliza Doolittle becomes a lady, as the best and most wonderful talents and attributes come to light. Discrimination is not a word in the Queen of Cups' dictionary. Because of this, she is sometimes viewed as too nice, too generous, eccentric, one who manages to get dumped on, and one always left holding the bag or cleaning up the mess. She is the one who applies the bandages, whether on a scratch, a broken heart or an injured psyche. Since each subject in her kingdom has wounds, the Queen of Cups makes it her business to heal as many of them as humanly possible. Don't question her ability to do it, for once she has made up her mind to accomplish a task, her tenacity in doing so is boundless.

How do you spell intuition? Did you say Q-u-e-e-n o-f C-u-p-s? You should have! Intuition is basic to all that she does, as well as all that she is. Her intuitive capacity is enormous, and her understanding of all situations makes dealing with a wide variety of people child's play. She reacts and interacts with each person on his or her own level and wavelength, instantly complimenting individual personality quirks. This chameleon-like ability allows her to get along with anyone and everyone. When 100 people are asked to describe her, 100 different descriptions will be forthcoming as each person sees her as a reflection of self. Sometimes the ability to change personas will actually confuse the Queen of Cups, even to the point of questioning her own nature and personality, but down at the core, she is a dreamer, a spiritualist, a magician, a healer. And on those points, she is secure with herself.

The Queen of Cups is generous to a fault, sometimes to her own detriment. She has little care for the material, and if cheated,

16

she would assume the person cheating needed the money or possession more than she did, instantly making the event a non-issue. Her thinking processes are much too advanced to waste time thinking about or re-hashing the trivial. She has a tendency toward introspection and is so at ease with her own thoughts that she often prefers her own company to the company of others. A combination of high psychic energy and constant introspective thought combine to keep her away from crowds and social situations. But when she does venture out into the public arena, her bright aura of open acceptance soon has her surrounded by those who can't help but be drawn to her.

PERSONALITY

By now you probably realize if you need to have a good cry, or just someone to lean on, the Queen of Cups is the ultimate shoulder provider. She wants and needs to be in control, especially in situations involving her personal business or the affairs of those she loves. Some might call her a control freak, and in essence, she is, but in the affairs of loved ones, she controls from a hidden place, orchestrating from behind the scenes. In this way she keeps the reins, but spares the feelings of her loved ones, allowing them to think they are doing it all on their own!

The Queen of Cups resents being told what to do; after all, as one of the oldest souls in the universe, she is much more experienced than the rest of the population. She has the wisdom of the ages within her and the experiences of an endless string of previous lives from which to draw knowledge. This enables her to know definitively what she wants and what she needs, and what to do to get it done. She may exhibit compulsive and perfectionistic behavior, not concerning all things, but only toward those things she deems important.

In addition to being the most sympathetic of listeners, the Queen of Cups is an excellent speaker. But don't ask her a question if you really don't want to hear the answer. She will tell you exactly what she thinks, even if you may find the answer unpleasant, though she will do so without hurting your feelings. As a true Royal, she is tactful if nothing else.

Her ability to adapt to any social situation makes her a natural as an actress or a writer (in fact, she is the designated journal keeper of the Tarot). But, she won't engage in any type of activity that doesn't produce results. Meaningless or time-wasting activities don't even make it onto her "to do" list. Her time is 100% productive; otherwise she is sleeping! It is extremely rare for the Queen of Cups to do something fun for the simple pleasure of the fun itself. It always has to be purposeful, and if it's fun, that's just a bonus.

In spite of her reserved personality, the Queen of Cups has a unique sense of self and absolute self-confidence. Like the beauty that walks in a room and turns everyone's head, she commands the attention of all in a room simply by entering it and can win over a room full of people at will with her seemingly magical charm.

And speaking of magic, or at least of all things spiritual, the Queen of Cups is an absolute believer in things magical and spiritual such as God, love potions, angels and fairy dust. Actually, the Queen of Cups is the most spiritual of the significators in the Tarot deck. She would never consider turning to the "dark side" because her faith in God is completely unshakable. She lives in firm confidence that God will take care of her and those she loves. Although she has no care for the material, she is fiercely passionate when it comes to injustice. She can overlook a plethora of others' idiosyncrasies, but if treated unfairly, the Queen of Cups may send up the battle standard and go to war. Once you have proven yourself unworthy of her time and attention, she will cut you off at the quick as though you no longer exist. She has an incredible memory, and once she has made the decision to cut you off as a person, she will not forget or rescind that decision.

Every coin has its flip side, and the significators of the Tarot are not exceptions to the rule. In the case of the Queen of Cups, there is a teensy little problem with addictive behavior. In times of extreme stress or crisis, she is likely to light up a cigarette, drink a cup of chamomile tea, wolf down a bag of cookies or a quart of Cherry Garcia, or just escape the stress by heading to bed. Strong psychic abilities have the Queen of Cups tuned in to the thought processes of everyone at all times. Mental health days were made for her, because sometimes she needs to turn it all off and just get away from everyone to relax.

And keep in mind that our Queen is a control freak, so if she tells you she's quit smoking those cigarettes, you will probably find a pack in her purse or drawer. Remember, in order to achieve control of situations, she has to be no less than a master manipulator, and what better way to manipulate than with occasional little white lies?

EMPLOYMENT

Because of her open-mindedness, the Queen of Cups is the most likely to read the Tarot. The cards speak to her. And, because of her ability to believe even the unbelievable, her interpretations are not jaded by reality or by the expected mores that taint readings attempted by others. Her strong psychic ability and uncanny intuition are her foremost tools and greatest assets.

When her inner voice speaks, she does well to listen, for even if she doesn't understand the why of it, her intuitive voice is never wrong. Not only does she read the feelings of others, but also her strong paranormal abilities enable her to communicate as well, usually without saying a word. She can make herself understood with a look, because she is looking straight into, and addressing, your soul.

Because of her "special" abilities, the Queen of Cups is wonderfully suited to any position that requires keenly developed interpersonal capability such as psychologist, actress, counselor, hair stylist or barber, social worker, bar tender, writer or librarian. Her metaphysical skills are unequaled. All her lifetimes worth of experience enables the Queen of Cups to dole out only the most sage and wise advice to those who need it.

But this same wealth of experience tends to have her jumping from job to job. She is multi-talented, and once she masters a task, she becomes bored and moves on to other challenges. She's also a procrastinator. It would not be out of character to hear her say, "It's not that I don't work well under pressure; it's that I ONLY work under pressure." Her life is a huge "last-minute" rush, but this does not seem to prevent her from meeting or exceeding her goals. Quite literally, she can and will achieve whatever she sets out to do.

Occupations that require a significant amount of travel are not very high on the list for a typical Queen of Cups. She is an inveterate nester, her home is her world, and she would much prefer to stay home surrounded by family and things familiar. As any Queen would be, she is best suited for a position of authority or as the owner and CEO of her own business concern. She loves a challenge, and her tendency to become bored easily makes her a restless, eager and dynamic business force.

APPEARANCE

The Queen of Cups is best described as a girly girl. She takes great care with her appearance and is well kept and acutely feminine, even in hiking boots and blue jeans. She loves surrounding herself with pretty things, and, as she likes soft scents (like flowers and springtime), her home is likely filled with potpourri, scented oils or burning incense. In looks, she is ageless. Her soft features and youthful glow give an appearance years younger than her actual chronological age--enough so to keep most people guessing. She is generally not an outdoors type, and you will rarely find her engaging in any activity that involves getting dirty or sweating. She is a Queen, after all, and no Queen would appear sweaty and dirty in any venue of her kingdom.

MONEY

A Queen of Cups will probably never be rich. She loves people more than money or the material and is likely to lavish all that she has on those people she cares for and loves. The means to riches are available to her, though money seems to find its way to her in strange and bizarre ways, such as the unexpected lottery win. But she is much happier giving it away than she is keeping it. She will always have what she wants and needs because her generous attitudes endow her with a Karma that keeps drawing more her way. If she wants a diamond bracelet or a pair of emerald earrings (and she always does), she will acquire them, but, never greedy, she only wants one of any item, not a dozen.

EMOTIONS

The Queen of Cups has an intensely emotional side. She loves water because it soothes her sensitive and intuitive soul. This includes water in all forms, be it swimming, walking by the ocean, taking showers, doing laundry or listening to relaxation CDs containing the sound of water or storms.

As a true psychic, the Queen of Cups will experience *deja vu* and prophetic dreams, and she will possess instinctive knowledge of what will come, even at a very early age. Her tendency to see what others cannot, and to speak of those things openly, often results in being labeled as eccentric or peculiar. But she is simply a person with gifts, marching to the beat of a different drum.

She loves deeply and totally and is intensely protective of those she loves. Our Queen is easily taken advantage of because of her almost endless tolerance and willingness to help others, but be aware that when she reaches her limit with someone, she closes the door and rarely, if ever, opens it again. She does have her anxious times because she is able to intuit even uncomfortable situations, but the mature Queen of Cups knows the strength of her spiritual energy will override any negative situation.

LOVE

The King of Wands is the perfect match for the Queen of Cups. He is a realist and she is a dreamer: a perfect balance for a long-term relationship. He is often chronologically older while she has the far older soul. This can be a great advantage to the Queen as an older man may help lighten the heaviness of the burdens she carries.

She wants and yearns to be held and cherishes affection in all its forms. Her children will often be gifts from of the house of Pentacles. Regardless of their suit, her children appreciate her and treat her with great love and respect.

The Queen of Cups is no slouch when it comes to handling men. While her mate may be older, she will always go for a younger lover. (Surprised? Even this Queen needs to play once in a while.) But any fling with a young lover won't last. She simply can't tolerate his constant energy and lack of responsibility for any length of time. But she leaves quite a lasting impression on any man she allows to enter her realm. Once he has been with her, he will never forget her, and will fondly and wistfully remember his time spent with the Queen.

When it comes to women friends, she does best with her earth sister in the Tarot, the Queen of Wands. But she also gets along famously with other Queens of Cups.

HEALTH

Her mind almost never turns off (it's part of her personality), and this gives our Queen a tendency toward depression and digestive problems. Her addictive behavior may result in unwanted weight gains, and she may develop thyroid problems or other hormonal imbalances. For the most part, she is generally healthy, and no major illness is common to her.

LEST WE FORGET

The Queen of Cups is an excellent gift giver. She knows her loved ones well and goes to great lengths to please them with her gift choices. Family antiques have great meaning for her (she is strongly attached to sentimental objects), and she'll only give them to people she feels will love and respect them as much as she does. Remember she values love over the material. If you are a good friend to a Queen of Cups, you might just be surprised one day when she gives you an extravagant gift, likely something she values and holds dear to her heart, such as a favorite piece of jewelry or a family heirloom. Accept it, enjoy it and treat it as something special, for very likely it is an article that could never be replaced.

And you may be struck by the Queen's love of music. There is almost always music of some kind wafting around in the background. She adores most forms of music and has very eclectic tastes. One minute she is listening to Mozart and the next to Rock and Roll. She may be blessed with musical or vocal ability, and if she is, she takes full advantage of it. If she is not so blessed, she just plays the music and hums along. She is happiest when melodic tones are filling her environment.

The Queen abhors war and violence and man's inhumanity to man. She will avoid news coverage of any event that glorifies or publicizes violent acts.

Last, but not least, her purse often looks like the inside of a garbage bag. It is where she keeps everything of importance. Her checkbook, credit cards, bills she doesn't want anyone to see, cards and letters that are sentimental to her, medications for every contingency, cell phone, address books, Band-Aids, emergency cash and endless other items she might "need" are in there. When her purse gets too heavy, she will empty it to remove the twenty dollars of spare change floating around on the bottom.

THE KNIGHT OF CUPS

THE BASICS:

- ♥ Also known as: The Jack of Hearts
- ♥ Sign: Tornado
- ♥ Flower: Foxglove
- ♥ Gemstone: Obsidian
- ♥ Characteristics: Manipulative, controlling, self-gratifying, charming
- ♥ Best Relationships: Queen of Wands, King of Wands, Queen of Cups
- ♥ Watchwords: "I need."
- ♥ Manifestations of the spirit world: Dreams, visions, scents, voices of the deceased

GENERAL

A tornado is the perfect representation of the Knight of Cups. Although fascinating as a personality, the Knight of Cups will blow into your life weaving a path of destruction and leaving emotional and financial shambles in his wake. Known as the Jack of Hearts in a regular deck, the Knight of Cups is the lovable rogue, the smiling scoundrel, the one most deserving of time in the bad-boy chair. Although he exudes charm, he uses it to manipulate and control both people and situations, and can quite literally talk anyone into doing anything. If there's a guy in the crowd urging some poor soul to drink another beer or to do something incredibly stupid, chances are, the Knight of Cups is that instigator. And about that "black sheep" in your family--you guessed it--more likely than not, he's a Knight of Cups. He is totally self-absorbed and the absolute antithesis of a family man.

The Knight of Cups often exhibits emotional and mental instability; of course, some Knights have a greater degree of that instability than others do. The cause can generally be traced back to dysfunctional family life during childhood. Although he appears to be a happy man with a devil-may-care attitude, he is not the good guy he seems to be. He is most at home pushing the limits of legality. Although the Knight is not normally violent, his criminal tendencies often find him driving without a license, dealing drugs, not paying his debts and stealing to bankroll his addictions.

For the most part, the Knight of Cups completely disregards rules and laws, preferring to live life on his own terms. The Knight never has a guilty conscience no matter what nastiness he has perpetrated, because he lacks the basic morals most of us were taught as children. It is almost as though he failed to reach the age of reason and has no concept of the difference between right and wrong.

PERSONALITY

There's no middle of the road when it comes to the character of the Knight of Cups. You'll either love him or hate him from the moment you meet him, and that first-impression feeling will last for the duration of your contact with him. Regardless of whether you feel love or hate toward him, he will cause windstorms of upheaval and unrest in your life. When young, the Knight of Cups is always the "problem" child, almost impossible to deal with on every conceivable level. He never outgrows his bad little boy complex, and he will never grow up. Like most spoiled children, the Knight is highly manipulative, and though he is smart as a whip, he uses his intellect only to con people and achieve personal gain at the expense of others. Oddly enough, his personality is especially appealing to older women, who, quite frankly, should know better. He knows exactly the type of woman to pursue: older women in need of flattery and young women with self-esteem problems who are overwhelmed by his professions of love. He tells them all exactly what they need to hear. It's just one of many ways he holds power over them.

The Knight of Cups is the epitome of an addictive personality, and his addictions are the driving forces in his life. Even though his most common addictions are drug and alcohol-related, he's addicted to many other things. He lives and feeds on his pleasures, including sex, gambling, using women, spending money, thrill seeking, etc. The Knight of Cups thinks all these things are his due, and woe is the person who dares to infringe on his pleasure. He becomes incensed if he feels his "right" to fun is being impinged on, but he has absolutely no compunction about denying someone else their rights. He will do what is necessary to have his way, once again with no conscience or guilt regarding the pain or consequences to others.

Don't be surprised if he seems to make himself at home in your house. He thinks nothing of using or taking anything he finds there. He has a "what's-yours-is-mine" attitude. He will proclaim to high heaven that he would do the same for you if your places were reversed, but that is simply his way of justifying his actions. Besides, your places will never be reversed; he is much too comfortable using you and your belongings for as long as you allow him to do so. He will never go out and do what is necessary to acquire such things in an honest and legitimate manner. He doesn't give much thought to how he can meet his needs and wants. He is much too busy scheming to get others to provide for him.

He just assumes that if he is welcome in your home, you won't mind at all if he takes or uses your things. Keep your belongings under lock and key if the Knight is coming for a visit, or you may just find that your things have walked out the door with your guest.

As you might imagine, the Knight of Cups is highly irresponsible. He tends to lie more often than he tells the truth, and is likely a pathological liar. Don't count on him for favors, but he may actually help you if it suits him. If you really need his help, just open your wallet. He'll do darn near anything for you if you are willing to pay him.

EMPLOYMENT

The best type of work for a Knight of Cups usually requires physical exertion. He is talented at any job he can do with his hands, such as mechanic, laborer, plumber or any blue-collar work. He is a hard worker, but only if and when it suits him. Most of the time he would rather be pursuing his pleasures. The Knight of Cups possesses an eye for detail that makes handwork easy, but it also makes it easier for him to be light-fingered and to carry out his criminal intentions.

APPEARANCE

Self-obsessed, narcissistic in the extreme, the Knight of Cups truly loves himself above all others. He thinks the way he looks, walks and talks is "cool." Except for his size (he is often small in stature), he thinks there is no one who looks or dresses better. His lack of height bothers him to a great degree, so he takes extra pains to make sure he is dressed and groomed in such a way as to distract others from noticing his lack of physical stature. This might mean he is buying and wearing designer clothes and sporting designer haircuts, but don't be surprised if he is multiply pierced and/or tattooed; he will do whatever he feels will best accomplish the task of directing attention away from his height.

If he bothers to work at all, he will be strong, muscular and full of vigor. If he is busy with his pleasures instead of keeping gainful employment, he will sometimes have a beer belly from his excesses. Generally he is young in mind and body.

MONEY

Forget long-term security. If you are involved with the Knight of Cups, be prepared for a day-to-day and hand-to-mouth existence. If and when he makes money, he has a very hard time not spending it all immediately. He puts his addictions before his responsibilities. He has no view of the big picture, seeing only those things that will make him happy right now. He might actually pay his bills for a month or two, but sooner or later he will be blowing the rent money on a new toy he just has to have or the grocery money on cigarettes and beer.

The Knight has absolutely no understanding of the concept of saving up to buy something he wants. Because of his pleasure addiction, he will always put his wants before his financial obligations. He is a thoughtless, reckless spender, never thinking twice about the needs of anyone other than himself. This leaves the burden of paying the bills and daily living expenses to his spouse, or whomever he happens to be mooching off of at the moment. This makes for disastrous family finances, especially if there are children involved. There is no financial security in a relationship with a Knight of Cups. A true indication of a Knight of Cups is the ability to acquire material things, but the inability to hold onto them.

EMOTIONS

Learning disabilities, hyperactivity and attention deficit disorder (ADD) are all very common in Knights of Cups. After exposure to the initial burst of charm, most people realize quickly that his behavior is erratic at best and, at worst, irrational. He can be almost manic at times, and he may use tranquilizers to keep himself grounded.

The Knight has a bit more psychic aptitude than most people do, but it is sometimes an untapped reservoir. His drug or alcohol use may impair that ability, and his ADD may not allow him to concentrate long enough to tap into that plane. Don't be surprised if he tells you stories of ghosts he has seen. He probably has, but as usual, he will embellish the story to the point of being more lies than truth. So take what he says with a grain of salt.

The Knight of Cups spends his lifetime using and manipulating other people. He has no use for anyone who is unable or unwilling to further his cause: the feeding of his addictions and pleasures. He is generally not vindictive, usually not intending to hurt people. He simply has no conscience, no guilt, and has no idea how much financial and emotional hurt and pain he inflicts on others in his quest for his own happiness.

LOVE

Love? Well, that isn't exactly what the Knight of Cups usually dishes up. He keeps a woman on his arm for status, for sex, and because having a woman feeds his addiction for pleasure.

Because of his charm, the Knight of Cups is appealing, particularly to older women. He makes them feel youthful and attractive and loved. He convinces them that they are special, and when an older woman is suddenly made to once again feel young and beautiful, she may have her vision clouded and her ability to discern the underlying deception disabled. This can be very dangerous, both emotionally and financially, for the woman involved. In an effort to keep the Knight happy and at her side, she may throw away a considerable amount of money in feeding his addictions. This is, of course, exactly what makes him happy, but the poor woman will end up just that: poor.

Many women want to love him, but if they have even a

modicum of dignity, their instinct for self-preservation prevents them from doing so. Unfortunately, women of all ages who suffer from lack of self-esteem will fall for his charm and flattery almost every time. The constant praise and adulation he bestows makes them feel positive about themselves and well loved, and they see him and view the ensuing relationship with rose-colored glasses.

The Knight of Cups is like a finicky houseplant that needs constant watering, but in his case, the care and feeding is in the form of money and emotional boosting. It is an esteem builder, to the woman who lacks esteem, to be needed in such a way, and so she will endlessly provide those components in the relationship. And since the Knight has radar for those who lack self-esteem, he can see such a woman coming from a mile away. He will drag her in and emotionally and monetarily bleed her to death if she doesn't wise up and get out while the going is good.

If (and this is a HUGE "if") the Knight of Cups ever grows up and settles down, his personality change will transform him into a King of Wands. It rarely happens before the age of 30, and in and in the case of hard drug use, it NEVER happens. For as long as he remains a Knight of Cups, his best romantic partner is the Queen of Wands. Her grounded nature may enable her to keep him under control (well, as much as can be managed), but only if she is a very emotionally strong and stable Queen of Wands. A strong Queen will nurture him without going over the line, and she will recognize crunch time and leave when the time comes. But if the Queen of Wands is suffering from self-esteem problems, he will chew her up, spit her out and leave her life in a complete shambles.

On the other end of the spectrum, the Queen of Pentacles is the worst match for a Knight of Cups. Because of her meticulous attention to detail and her goal-oriented personality, she would most likely end up with a nervous condition if she had to tolerate the Knight's complete lack of responsibility and lackadaisical attitude. A romantic liaison between them would result in a disaster of catastrophic proportions on an emotional level for the

Queen of Pentacles, while the Knight would say "Oh, well" and begin looking for his next meal ticket.

The Queen of Cups might start a relationship with the Knight, but once she realizes what she is in for, she will exit with all the speed she can muster.

Regardless of Tarot specific characteristics, any woman who is considering a relationship with a Knight of Cups needs to keep in mind that monogamy is NOT one of his long suits. More often than not, the Knight of Cups is sexually promiscuous. He plants his seed and moves on, often siring dozens, but not assuming responsibility for any. Promiscuity fits his addicted personality like a glove, feeding his ego and filling his need for his next bit of pleasure. And remember, he has absolutely no guilt about being promiscuous, so don't expect him to mend his ways anytime soon.

HEALTH

In health, as in all things, the Knight of Cups is always his own worst enemy. He drinks too much, sometimes eats too much and never gives a thought to the long-term effects of his addictive behavior. He is also a risk taker and thrill seeker. In his quest for pleasure, he has acquired a taste for the adrenaline rush, and so pushes well beyond his own physical capability, often injuring himself in the process. Like a cat with nine lives, he likes to show off and walk the top of the alley fence, often just one step away from death.

LEST WE FORGET

The Knight of Cups is not mean spirited. He doesn't intend to inflict hurt or pain. But he feels no guilt about the results of his actions. He is underhanded and sneaky and prefers that someone else be the breadwinner and support him. When he loses his free ride with one woman, he will often return to the scene of the crime and attempt to get an old flame to take him back. He will do anything to avoid supporting himself.

THE KING OF PENTACLES

KING of PENTACLES.

THE BASICS:

- ♦ Also known as: The King of Diamonds
- ♦ Sign: Gold
- ♦ Flower: Dogwood
- ♦ Gemstone: Black Diamond
- ♦ Characteristics: Striking, inspires confidence, educated, money-oriented
- ♦ Best Relationships: Queen of Wands, King of Wands
- ♦ Watchwords: "I will take over from here."
- ♦ Manifestations of the spirit world: Sounds, hearing

GENERAL

You find your way into a dark cave by the soft glow of your flashlight. The room opens to you, and you survey your surroundings. Everywhere there are piles of radiant solid gold ingots, and you stand and stare in awe. The power, the allure, the feelings of success and wealth you are experiencing are indicative of the persona of the King of Pentacles. He is a striking figure. He exudes and inspires confidence. The King is always well educated, about 95% have college degrees. If he is one of the remaining 5% who did not have the advantage of obtaining a college education, he may feel somewhat embarrassed that he does not hold a degree, even though his self-education is more than adequate. Often, as the result of his generosity and philanthropic efforts, he is awarded honorary degrees from the most prestigious universities.

The King of Pentacles loves the power that money can buy, and the material things it can buy as well. He can be exceedingly magnanimous in his giving, especially if it puts him in a good light and advances his business concerns. It is essential that he have enough money to acquire the accouterments of a wealthy life style. This need makes the King of Pentacles a driven, career-oriented individual. He is the very successful workaholic.

As a young man, it is likely that he obediently followed the path dictated by his parents. He attended college, started a financially rewarding career, and married an attractive, socially acceptable and socially conscious wife, who was absolutely certain she snagged the catch of the century. He bought a starter home that was the envy of his peers, but then realized he had to cough up the bucks to pay for all the trappings of success he was sure he needed.

The result of this path is the plot line of countless books and movies. The wonderful well-meaning husband and father becomes a workaholic, spending increasingly more time at his job, 14 to 16 hour days. Home time is used for reviewing and preparing for whatever comes next. The extent of his recreation is weekend golf, but only with business contacts, because advancing his business is his uppermost goal.

He is very likely to pick up the tab, especially if it will advance his successful image or is beneficial to his business interests. He knows that putting forth a successful image will create success and he is more than willing to employ the "spend money to make money" theory.

PERSONALITY

The King of Pentacles is a warm and communicative human being. He can talk to anyone at any level. He is humorous, keen-witted and fun to spend time with, if he will actually allot the time to be with you. The King is very goal-oriented, living his life from one achieved goal to the next. He is a driven personality; if he had no goals to strive for he would be lost. The King is very adept at playing the game, and he always plays to win. He is a natural leader, who always has direction and is decisive enough for the masses to follow. A work-obsessed over achiever, the King goes happily along in life chasing the ever-larger payday. He cares for his family and works to give them everything they want, eventually to his own detriment. He is obsessed with earning the almighty dollar, but has no problem giving it away. The King of Pentacles is an ardent philanthropist; he believes money will fix anything. He is not usually an alcoholic personality, but alcohol plays a very large role in his lifestyle because it is a social smoother and a stress buster.

EMPLOYMENT

Most of what can be said about the King of Pentacles fits in this category. His life is his work and his work is his life. He must always rise to the top; as a result he can be very aggressive in the business world. You are most likely to find the King of Pentacles at the top of any corporation. He is the president, the vice-president, the CEO, the CFO. He may be found in banking, sales, finance and brokerage firms, but he is just as likely to pick marketing or advertising, because they are also high-powered, big money and big budget careers (can you say, demanding, unforgiving, fast-paced and high-stress jobs?).

The King of Pentacles is inevitably his own harshest critic. He creates challenges for himself at lifetime rate that exceeds the challenges of all the other Kings of the Tarot combined. He is the quintessential communicator, a master of languages, his own and others. Often he is multi-lingual, which enables him to communicate with potential business contacts on an international level. He has the ability to size up any individual and immediately communicate at as high or as low of a level as is required to speak to the intellect of that person and win their confidence and trust. He uses that ability to reach into the heart and soul of that person and make himself completely understood. This innate gift of winning people over gives the King of Pentacles a huge advantage. He can enter a totally untenable situation and use his powers of persuasion to come out on top; he succeeds where others fail. Some may view this as manipulative behavior, but it is far from that. The King of Pentacles believes in himself and his ability, and when he sells himself to someone it is with honesty and integrity. He will fulfill his promises because not to come through with what was promised would reflect poorly on him.

Once committed to any project, the King of Pentacles will throw himself into the fray with all he's got. Like a pit bull with its teeth in someone's leg, he will tenaciously work to make the project productive, efficient and profitable. It is virtually impossible to separate him from his work until success is achieved.

Some may think that his obsession with career is totally irresponsible. The truth is that he is acting with the best of intentions. He is working for the financial security of his family, and really believes that he is doing his best and giving his all for their welfare. But like King Midas, he doesn't realize that money is not the be all and end all. He is totally unaware that while he is out making a name for himself, grooming his reputation and making money to afford all the things he feels are necessary to keep up with the upper crust, his family is suffering from his total lack of attention.

APPEARANCE

The King of Pentacles is always well groomed, squeaky clean and looking like a successful professional. He dresses for success because he knows that putting forth the correct image will put him at an advantage in the business world. He buys the best clothes, shoes and accessories. He wears fine leathers, silks and wool; goes to an expensive hair stylist, not a barber; and purchases only top-of-the-line colognes and personal products.

MONEY

Money is what the King of Pentacles is all about. Quite frankly he is loaded. He drives a Corvette or a Lexus or Ferrari. He wears $2500 tailored suits and $300 casual pants and thinks nothing of spending that much for clothing just for the name on the tag. He makes money by his creative work efforts, experience and know-how. He is wise with his investments. If you buy the stocks he's buying, you'll soon have a tidy nest egg!

EMOTIONS

Regardless of his truly good intentions, the King of Pentacles' obsession with wealth drives away the very family he is trying so hard to provide for with his idea of life's necessities. He would never leave them, and does not understand why they are unhappy enough to leave him. He is genuinely devastated by the loss of his family, usually vowing never to marry again. The King is far too set in his ways by the time this occurs to make the changes necessary to repair the situation. And he is usually not quite finished building his empire at this point in time. He really doesn't know any other way to live, and he doesn't know or want to know how to change the person he has become.

He will give as much time to the children, after the fact, as possible, but soon he is back to his old ways, using work not only to attain his goals but also to numb the pain of his loss. He is unhappy, but content to make work his mistress. He knows she will never leave him. He is a compassionate man, especially as he gets on in age and begins to learn that people are more important than gold.

The King of Pentacles lives under the cloud of money, and equates providing money and material things with holding up his end of the relationship. The King is stunned by personal loss, and is very insecure after his first initial heartbreak. He is lonely without being alone, and acutely sensitive to the needs of others.

LOVE

The King of Pentacles doesn't understand that love is more than just giving "things" to his family. He works long hours to provide for them rather than spending any quality time with them. While he is obsessed with earning more money, his children are wondering why their father is the one never there for school functions and sporting events. He is oblivious to the fact that providing his children with the best athletic equipment, best summer camps, latest and greatest in gadgets and toys, and their own credit cards is not an adequate substitution for the attention of their father. They may even make endless trips to the Limited or the Lands End Store with that Master Card just to make him pay for his lack of day-to-day love and concern. The sad thing is that they learn, much faster that he, that money isn't everything.

The wife of the King of Pentacles is in for a rude awakening. She married him with grand designs for living a high-class and privileged life. And she does indeed live the high life. She moves in the best circles, belongs to right social and civic groups. She wears the latest in designer cloths, drives a luxury car and owns a veritable wardrobe of jewelry. She takes annual cruises to get away and is likely to have in her employ a cleaning service and a personal trainer at the minimum. But in spite of all the wealth and privilege she is often unhappy. The

King of Pentacles' wife craves close, personal, daily contact with the man she loves. She feels neglected and learns that all the "things" she has are not a good substitute. This is especially true of a King of Pentacles and his wife if they have come up the ladder from the average middle-class arena. Those that ascend to the wealthier echelon, rather than being born into it, know that there is a different, calmer way of living, and they sometimes need and yearn for the familiarity of the middle-class comfort zones. The King's wife will look back longingly to the days of Sunday breakfast in bed, dinner at Grandma's house, playing with the kids, talking and making love through the night, planting a flower garden together--all the things she feels she is missing.

She longs for the physical contact and intimacy most of all and, eventually, she will seek it elsewhere. All the material wealth in the world won't make up for the lack of human touch. The King of Pentacles becomes just like King Midas destroying those he loves because he can no longer touch them.

HEALTH

The King of Pentacles is a very driven, money-obsessed man. He often suffers from Workaholic Syndrome, the signs of which are hypertension, ulcers, gastritis, tension headaches, anxiety and depression. He is often on blood pressure and antidepressant medications to control symptoms he wouldn't have if he just slowed down and spent more time away from work and doing fun family things.

LEST WE FORGET

When the King of Pentacles loses his family, it seldom involves another woman. After the loss, the King will often spend many years alone, using his work as a substitute for family. Once he reaches his ultimate financial goals and acquires the wisdom of years, he may discover that he has many other interests to pursue. His overabundance of creative energy will be thrown into areas such as the arts. He discovers theater, plays, music and travel and will suddenly become a season subscriber. The King will enroll in art classes, learning to paint and sculpt. He will begin spending time in creative writing or learning to play the guitar or piano. In similar fashion, he will also increase his interest in community events, buying season tickets to the local NFL and MLB teams and actually using them as recreation rather than business catapults.

As he gets older, late forties-early fifties, he starts seriously thinking about the loneliness of growing old without a loving partner. He will endeavor to seek out a new partner, and he will eventually find one. The second wife of the King of Pentacles will be blessed. Now that his obsession with work has waned and he realizes the time he has wasted, he will shower her with all the time, love and attention he can give. This will be coupled with extreme generosity. He earned it, he has it to give, and he will spend it freely on his new wife and family members. The nice thing is that he will do it with love, not as a substitution for his attention. So wife number two gets the best of both worlds. She is one very lucky woman.

The aging King of Pentacles gets a vicarious thrill out of watching his loved ones open a new gift. He, like King Midas of legend, finally learns that gold is not the be all and end all of life. He learns that the most important thing of all is the love of good people and having someone to share your life and your wealth. Otherwise it was all for nothing.

THE QUEEN OF PENTACLES

QUEEN ⬧ PENTACLES

THE BASICS:

- ◆ Also known as: The Queen of Diamonds
- ◆ Sign: Swan
- ◆ Flower: Rose
- ◆ Gemstone: Diamond
- ◆ Characteristics: Logical, analytical, creative
- ◆ Best Relationships: Knight of Pentacles, King of Wands, King of Pentacles
- ◆ Watchwords: "Let me organize my thoughts."
- ◆ Manifestations of the spirit world: Sounds, hearing

GENERAL

Can you think of anything more graceful, more elegant, than a solitary swan on a mirror-like pool of water? This would be an appropriate vision of the Queen of Pentacles, who carries herself in just that way, perfectly poised and gliding through life in one seemingly effortless motion. But don't let the serenity of the scene fool you, because she isn't really floating at all. Under that smooth, shimmering surface, her feet are stuck like glue to the bottom.

There are many paths to becoming a significator, and the Queen of Pentacles generally takes one of three main roads to her royal demeanor. She may be born to it. Some queens are born as, and always remain, Queens of Pentacles. Some queens grow into it. We learn what we live with and then either emulate our role models or disassociate ourselves from them. A Queen of Pentacles is likely to have a mother who was a helper, a fixer, a social worker; a mother who was so busy helping everyone else that she had limited time for her parental obligations. The Queen of Pentacles will go to extremes in an effort to not emulate such a mother, and in becoming the opposite of her mother, gains Queen of Pentacles stature. The third road is frustration. Many times a Queen of Pentacles is a converted Queen of Cups. Frustrated with playing the role of the nurturing pushover, she eventually declares the need to do things just for herself, deliberately changing to break free of her former identity. But no matter how she got there, the Queen of Pentacles is completely and totally grounded in reality. She is a goal setter who not only sets "realistic and attainable" goals but meets or exceeds those goals consistently.

PERSONALITY

She is a planner, an organizer, and a logical, analytical thinker. The Queen of Pentacles is the one to call when you need help to plan or organize any function from a family picnic to a massive corporate or governmental event. She has a penchant for

41

sorting out every minute detail and maintaining an organized way of dealing with the briars that pop up to threaten the schedule. She will accurately advise you on how to go about achieving any goal. Not only will this Queen sort out the details and give you terrific advice; she'll give you step-by-step instructions for attaining your goal. The path she outlines for you will always be the correct one, because in logical and analytical fashion, she has thought through every possible scenario and every result no matter how improbable.

She needs her life to be in good order and avoids chaos like the plague. Most of the time she succeeds, at least in her career. Be assured that when she advises you, she will give you a plan that emulates her professional life. But, strangely enough and through no fault of her own, chaos is common in her non-professional life, especially in her close personal relationships. What she really wants in a man is someone exactly like herself, but she is prone to choosing partners who have only a veneer of being orderly and stable. Once she discovers that the veneer is nothing but camouflage for many personality and emotional problems, she will work to divest herself of the relationship, causing upheaval in her personal life. This unwelcome and unwanted personal chaos is highly distressing to the Queen, and she will work ten times harder to restore and maintain order and calm. Because of the chaos in her relationships, she is fastidious about keeping order and organization in the other parts of her life.

The wheels in the Queen of Pentacle's logical mind never stop turning. Even when she appears to be relaxing she is still planning and thinking. Her amazingly goal-oriented personality makes her somewhat of a workaholic. She craves safety and security, and she will work like the devil to get things done, even before the tasks need to be finished. But she is not completely devoted to her job, even though she attacks her duties with zeal and perfectionism. She works at work, but she also works at play! The Queen has an affinity for dealing with children and a deep-seated love of games and brainteasers. She can often be found cross-legged on the floor playing board games or cards with the kids as though she is still a kid herself.

As mentioned previously, the Queen of Pentacles is the perfect person to seek out when you need counsel or advice, and don't concern yourself over lack of confidentially, because the Queen of Pentacles is not the gossiping type. There's no need to worry that your deep dark secrets or personal information will be freely available across the back fence. She's also a great motivator, and if you're depressed, you can bet she'll lift you up out of that hole you're in, BUT (and it's a big one), she has little patience for those who create their own problems. She sees a huge difference between one who is depressed as a victim of circumstance and one who is depressed from wallowing in self pity and refusing to do anything about it, even when capable of doing so.

Although the Queen may seem aloof, stuck up or snobby, she's really just a little bit shy. As mentioned, it is quite likely that she had a mother who had time for everyone else and little time for her daughter. Her mother was the type who felt it was her calling to give and do for anyone needing her help, to a great degree beyond what most people would consider judicious. Because of her mother's magnanimous giving of her time and attention to others, our queen may have felt neglected. Determined not to become her mother, she will limit herself to helping only those people close to her. She is intent on having a life of her own and will not let her sympathetic feelings for others dissuade her from her goals and plans. That is not to say she is selfish, she most certainly isn't. She just doesn't want to deal with the mundane aspects of living a totally giving life. Therefore, she chooses to bestow help on only a chosen few while guarding and valuing her "me" time.

EMPLOYMENT
The Queen of Pentacles is a multi-faceted, multi-talented

individual. It really doesn't matter what type of work she chooses, because she'll excel at whatever she tries. If she goes with her strengths, she will stick to managerial and administrative jobs. Her superb organizational skills would hold her in good stead in a research position, or any job that involves lots of detail and planning. Those same skills make her a good candidate for any job that involves transactions, such as banking, telecommunications, financial advice or real estate sales. She would also be good in the medical field, as she has the talent, intelligence and the organizational tools to achieve a medical degree with no problem. Just remember, given the opportunity, the Queen of Pentacles could efficiently run the world. Her communication skills would make her a first-rate diplomat or ambassador. Her artistic ability may lead her into the media or graphic design.

APPEARANCE

Remember the swan at the beginning of this chapter? The Queen of Pentacles is exactly like that swan, a regal presence among the common fowl. She is a classic example of good breeding, regardless of her parental background. It doesn't matter whether she is wearing jeans or a formal gown; she always looks exquisite and elegantly dressed. The Queen of Pentacles would not be caught dead in public without her make-up. She must always look fresh and perfect. She carries herself well, moving in a smooth, coordinated way, and is quite literally always the epitome of grace. She will often wear diamonds, and they are always high quality and tasteful in design. She would never appear gaudy, but always understated and classic.

MONEY

There is no other queen more likely to become wealthy than the Queen of Pentacles. Her unequaled organizational skills will enable her to invest any windfall and ensure happiness and monetary security for herself and her family. Even if she's never had two nickels to rub together in the past, she will study, research and organize to make sure that such a treasure is wisely invested. Those same organizational skills may enable the Queen of Pentacles to land a position that pays well. She spends what is necessary to fill her needs, and the rest she saves and wisely puts to work toward a comfortable and secure financial future. But she loves personal frivolities and wants the best of everything. She will do what is necessary to insure that she can have the things she desires. She may get a second job to earn enough money to feed her need to buy those expensive things, or she may make additional investments. But never one to not use all the resources at her disposal, she may just save herself a lot of effort and find a rich lover.

EMOTIONS

Emotions can be the bane or the pride of her existence. Although the Queen of Pentacles is often an emotional mess personally, she has no problem doling out excellent advice when others need help with their emotional troubles. Once again, her ability to organize, plan and think things through makes her advice some of the best that can be found. And her advice will be rock solid, dead on, and firmly grounded in reality, so it is best to listen well and heed her wisdom. She will never send you off on some wayward tangent. The closest distance between two points is a straight line, and she will advise you of the line to follow. If you take her advice, you will succeed. It is as simple as that.

Although she has no problems talking to others about their emotional upheavals, the Queen of Pentacles is highly sensitive about the things she views as her own personal shortcomings. She is not at all comfortable discussing her emotions or feelings openly. Many times she doubts her own personal judgment. Often, she will do what she thinks others expect her to do rather than what she really wants to do. This only adds to her own emotional turmoil. She would be much better off to act as her swan, floating off where she will, a freeing of the spirit that

45

would give her psyche enormous relief from its self-inflicted stresses. She is highly emotional by nature, and sublimating her own needs to act as she thinks others want her to act only creates a bottle-neck of emotions. And we all know that bottled-up emotions are both physically and emotionally damaging.

Her organized side really hates any disruptions in her life. She works hard at being a dutiful person, daughter, mother, etc. She always remembers birthdays, anniversaries and other milestone events in the lives of the people she feels close to, and she always makes a gesture of remembrance such as an appropriate card or gift.

Although she can be overly analytical, every Queen of Pentacles is an artist at heart. Music, writing, painting and pursuing beauty are necessary channels of release to keep her emotions in balance. Her creative beast is best set loose on home decorating, creative clothing, and stunning makeup. She may also do some creative sewing, functional things that are also beautiful, such as quilts. She loves to surround herself with beautiful things, flowers (especially roses), paintings, unique décor, and designer clothing. She is in essence an elegant and beautiful creature living in a beautiful world of her own design.

LOVE

Of course, much of the personal turmoil in the otherwise orderly life of the Queen stems from her relationships. Her judgment is normally exceptional, and her intelligence and analytical thinking lead her to choosing an appropriate mate. However, many Queens of Pentacles will use poor judgement choosing the right person, especially when lacking the wisdom of age. For some reason she has no instinct about who is right for her. As a result she will date one loser after another and may eventually marry one. There is a good possibility that she will have a life-altering experience in her quest for a good mate. Because of that bad experience, she will finally learn to discern who is right for her and who is not. She will become infinitely more choosy about the men she chooses to date. After the first divorce, she will not make the same mistake again. When she finally finds the right man it will be a life-long relationship. But it won't happen until later in her life. Once rid of the first marriage, she will devote herself to making a perfect home and family life for her children. The Queen would never allow her children to suffer from her repeated bad choices in men, and has no desire to heap more hurt upon her soul. Of course, she is certain only she knows what is best for her kids and will not expose them to anyone she considers "questionable". Therefore, she will stay single and emotionally unavailable until the time is right to make another change. But she will remarry, if and only if, she finds a man that will put her first and will care for her children as his own. Otherwise, when she is satisfied that the children are grown and can make it on their own in the world, she will set about finding a companion, lover and mate for the rest of her life.

Her ideal mate is the King of Pentacles, and her best friends are fellow Queens of Pentacles or Queens of Cups. Although she's attracted to men with money and power (she's somewhat of a power groupie), she has trouble hanging on to them for any length of time. She is not likely to make the final commitment unless she is absolutely positive that things will work out. This is fueled by the tight control she keeps over her emotions. The unruly Knight of Cups is her worst possible choice. He is always full of childish games, and the Queen of Pentacles simply can't be bothered with him. If she becomes "involved" with the Knight of Cups, her life will be one of abject misery until she ends the relationship.

HEALTH

The Queen of Pentacles is generally very healthy. She works hard at keeping herself that way with exercise and a moderate diet. However, she may be burdened with stress-related illnesses such as headaches and tight muscles. It is usually nothing so severe that a little ibuprofen and a good massage can't effect a cure, and she will seek and use such remedies. She feels best when exercising, so it is a good idea for her to invest in some home exercise equipment, join a gym, or simply take regular walks. If done on a regular basis, this will also help to relieve the amount of stress she brings on herself. Many of these Queens suffer from problems with the reproductive organs.

LEST WE FORGET

The Queen of Pentacles is an avid list maker. She can live and die by her lists and will accomplish all that she sets out to do by following her plan. She always writes checks and is never late paying her bills or making a scheduled appointment.

A collector of just about anything that's pretty, she always buys the best of whatever she is buying. She pampers herself, and denies herself little. She always sports good haircuts and styles, has professional manicures, frequents tanning booths and takes vacations in the best spots. She treats herself to designer clothing and accessories such as leather handbags and expensive jewelry. And she takes exceptional care with her possessions so she can pass them down to her children in immaculate and pristine condition.

She has high expectations for herself and for her children. She encourages her kids in the arts and sports and guides them to become well-rounded individuals. She is a proponent of education in all aspects and raises her children to be neat and well mannered. Her children are usually fellow Pentacles and are often praised for their politeness around strangers.

The Queen of Pentacles is not averse to traveling alone. She enjoys the freedom to explore as she chooses, unfettered by the demands of a companion.

Last but not least, the Queen of Pentacles is a closet romantic. She needs and craves attention from her mate (or if she has no mate, her suitors). She needs regular tokens of affection such as flowers, cards, diamonds and travel, otherwise she feels sullen and grumpy. When she is alone she fantasizes often about her mate or suitors. She may even think in French. She is very choosy about friends and keeps only a small circle of trusted ones within her reach.

THE KNIGHT OF PENTACLES

KNIGHT of PENTACLES

THE BASICS:

♦ Also known as: The Jack of Diamonds
♦ Sign: Dolphin
♦ Flower: Gladiola
♦ Gemstone: Sapphire
♦ Characteristics: Intelligent, analytical, organized
♦ Best Relationships: Queen of Pentacles, Queen of Cups, Knight of Pentacles
♦ Watchwords: "I believe it would be better if we did it this way."
♦ Manifestations of the spirit world: Sounds, hearing

GENERAL

The symbol of human intelligence and caring in the realm of marine life, the dolphin has for centuries been portrayed as the savior at sea, rescuing humans in distress. It is the perfect sign for the Knight of Pentacles, whose intelligence is unmatched, and whose humanity is such that he is the proverbial knight in shining armor. The Jack of Diamonds in a regular deck, the Knight of Pentacles has all the qualities necessary to be successful.

A master of all forms of communication (well, maybe not echolocation), the Knight is an expert persuader. His writing and speaking talent enables him to sway entire crowds. His ability to persuade is second to none. He has an extensive vocabulary, and he has an endless capacity for translation of feelings into words with almost measurable accuracy.

Just like the dolphin, the savior of the sea, the Knight of Pentacles will appear in your life out of the blue, when you least expect him, but when you need him most. His presence and influence will dramatically change your life in untold numbers of ways. Your whole concept of self-knowledge, every last feeling and perception you have about your life, will be altered for the better by his presence. When his purpose for coming into your life is complete, he will disappear into the depths of his own goal-orientated life, like the dolphin disappears into the depths of the ocean.

The Knight of Pentacles is the perfect example of an intellectual giant. He is the Gulliver of brains, and the rest of us are but Lilliputians by comparison. The Knight of Pentacles is the most intelligent card of the Tarot. And to make the picture a little sweeter, he is also the most verbal, interesting, humorous, and sensitive of the Knights. Sit back and be amazed, as he astonishes you with myriad talents and abilities.

PERSONALITY

A keen wit and a sense of humor are always indicative of an active and developed mind. As the most intelligent card in the

Tarot, it generally follows that the Knight of Pentacles is sharp-witted and funny. Don't be surprised if, in the middle of serious conversation, he suddenly says something witty. He uses well-placed humorous comments to command the audience and draw people back to the points he is trying to make.

The Knight of Pentacles is a logical analytical thinker who thinks things through and knows that keeping his eye on the goal will get him there faster. He is consistent, progressive and goal-oriented in his work habits. He plans ahead, then sticks to the plan to realize his goals. He has a firm and sure idea of where he is going in life. That is not to say he won't deviate from the straight and narrow now and again. However, the plan is the plan, and whatever stops or side trips he makes along the way will not be of a nature that prevents him from achieving his goal. They are but minor delays to gaining knowledge and enriching his intellectual processes.

The Knight of Pentacles truly likes himself and appreciates the talents and abilities with which he is blessed. Although he certainly has reason to feel superior and act like an egomaniac, he is far from being egotistical. He is a down-to-earth person with a cerebral mentality, and he requires and pursues activities that stimulate his thinking. He is easily bored and hungers for new ideas and new information. The Knight does spend some time each day exploring his own mental abilities and fascinates even himself at times. But is it not just his innate intelligence that makes the Knight of Pentacles so very wise. He also has the ability to view life from many perspectives and can communicate with all people, regardless of intellectual level. His ability to put himself in another's shoes allows him to see things from another's point of view. He can then take action or dispense advice based on that viewpoint. He can literally become a person, know what that person is thinking, and use his gift to bring out the very best in that person to accomplish the desired results.

The Knight of Pentacles can relate to strangers and make friends with anyone. His intelligence and humor are wide ranging.

If he is confronted by a topic about which he knows little, he will seek the information, researching the topic until he is satisfied that he has acquired the appropriate knowledge. Once that knowledge is available and absorbed, the Knight will never forget what he has learned. His mind is like a steel trap. Information flows in, and his brain's disk space is unlimited. His intellect is amazing. He has but to hear, read or see something once and it becomes a permanent addition to his cranial disk storage. In the rare circumstance that a Knight of Pentacles has a learning disability, he will still retain and test out higher than the average person.

Always seeking a new experience and more knowledge, the Knight of Pentacles loves to travel, but travel is loosely defined. He may or may not appreciate physical travel. Not minding if it is by choice, but possibly resenting it if the travel is frequent and required. Mind travels are a favorite. His creativity allows him to get lost in an activity or experience and relish it as though it were a physical trip, be it lost in a song, a movie or a book. The Knight of Pentacles loves to listen to music; his car radio or CD player is always on while he's driving. He likes music that means something to him and is not into trendy pop music or spoiled teen rock stars. If a book or movie really moves him, he will be thinking and talking about it for a long time. He is not easily impressed with the latest movie or best seller. It has to be really good to make such an impact on him.

The Knight of Pentacles is also a creature of habit. He is comfortable in his own world, in his own surroundings amongst familiar things. If his world is disturbed, be it his work world or his personal life, he will use his incredible ability to communicate to express his irritation, often verbally brutalizing the person who dared to upset his apple cart. There is no question that he can easily put someone in his or her place. He is amazingly good at doing so and won't hesitate for a moment if he feels it is deserved.

If it is really stellar advice you are seeking, the Knight of Pentacles is the perfect person to ask. His wisdom is second to none. He is a realist, and his ability to see everyone's point of view makes him an excellent mediator. He will do everything he can to smooth out disputes between, or involving, his loved ones. And he will not betray a confidence. No matter what you tell him, it goes no further, even if he is hearing things from both sides in a dispute. He is generally a thoughtful person, but even more so if it suits his needs in getting ahead.

EMPLOYMENT

The Knight is an excellent teacher, blessed with verbal and communication skills that make communicating with youth a very simple task. But he is also a perfectionist. He gets things done the right way, the first time and without wasting any time; he expects everyone else to do the same. Naturally it causes him stress to watch the world going on its way without meeting his strict work ethic. The Knight of Pentacles is also an excellent writer and speaker, so you may find him as an award-winning journalist or successful politician. It is essential that his chosen path give him adequate opportunities for advancement, because he is constantly seeking to go for the gold.

He always does a great job, regardless of career, but he expects to be well paid for his services. If he is underpaid, he is very unhappy and will not last long in that position. He doesn't mind doing physical labor, but he knows his capabilities and would much rather earn a living with his intellect. Don't be surprised to find him in a program manager's position. His perfectionism and ability to think analytically make him perfect for any job that involves planning and organization. A Knight of Pentacles is usually the one pulling all the organizational strings for any large building project or scheduling people, products and projects for a major corporation. But he is also likely to partner or run his own business. He needs to be at the top, or reaching for it, regardless of his avocation.

APPEARANCE

The Knight of Pentacles is meticulous about his appearance. His clothing is always high quality, clean and pressed. Yes, he does own an iron! He likes top of the line clothing and is not a discount-shopping fan. When he buys something, he buys the very best he can afford. And he dresses very conservatively, even when he is still a young man. Always conscious of his personal hygiene, he has a neat, trimmed hairstyle, and beard or mustache if he sports one, getting professionally trimmed on a regular basis. It is fascinating to watch a Knight of Pentacles become an adult. He may have sported dread locks or waist-length hair and done wild and crazy things in high school or college, but once he gets into the real world, the dread locks, long hair and wild times are gone and a conservative but ambitious businessman takes his place.

MONEY

The Knight of Pentacles was born to be rich. He likes the lifestyle and needs to maintain his persona. But he doesn't expect wealth to be handed to him on a platter. He knows that he will get what he wants by working for it, and has a very high standard of work ethic. The Knight is not afraid to demand the pay and perks that are commensurate with his experience and abilities. But he does seem to fall into good money positions, and those positions come to him quickly. It is not unusual for him to change jobs every year or so while he is still young and unattached, and each change will dramatically raise his income level. He generally does not squander his money, but he can be incredibly generous with his loved ones. When he does want to purchase something, as with his clothing, it is always the best he can buy and, rather impatiently, he wants it yesterday.

EMOTIONS

Creativity and sensitivity are almost always found in the same package. Surprisingly, the intelligent, analytical, organized and conservative Knight of Pentacles is also highly sensitive and very creative. As a child, he was filled with fantasy, with a powerful drive to the imaginary. He learned to "become" other characters, which is the basis of his ability to see all perspectives through the eyes of others. He learned to love the arts early on in life and may be blessed with largely untapped artistic ability. Participating in school programs or plays gave him an outlet to legitimately change personalities--more practice for his future communications talent. He will change roles as needed to achieve whatever his current goal may be at the time. And he always has a goal, even when very young. The Knight will do what is necessary to achieve that goal and will not stop until he succeeds. He will already have another goal in mind and immediately sets his intellect and resources on the new path.

The Knight of Pentacles is extremely empathetic to the needs of others, but only if their needs are legitimate. He has no patience or tolerance for those who ruin their own lives and then whine and cry about their misfortune. He plans; therefore, he expects everyone else to plan for their own future and for the unexpected roadblocks and glitches that may arise. Empathy not withstanding, the Knight has no need or desire to be a fixer of people. His logic will not allow him to waste his resources in such a way, but he will be supportive and loving while they fix themselves. Wallowing in self-pity turns him off like a light switch.

Continually needing mental stimulation and additional experiences, the Knight of Pentacles is endlessly curious and will participate in very divergent activities. He is never afraid to try something new and different. But he always thinks things through before taking action. His mind is sharp and logical, preventing him from going off half cocked in his activities.

The Knight of Pentacles has a strong belief in God and a quiet faith. He is not one to believe in the paranormal or in fairies, ghosts, Tarot cards or psychics. He considers all those things to be ridiculous hocus-pocus nonsense. The Knight has complete faith in himself and believes that he can accomplish all goals through the power of his intellect and appropriate planning. In his heart, he believes if he uses the talents God gave him, that God will always take care of him. His attitude is akin to "God helps those who help themselves". He is rather close-mouthed about his beliefs, never advertising them and considering them to be highly personal. The Knight can also be very stubborn, and dissuading him from his beliefs is virtually impossible. But since he has thought out every possible outcome, every angle of attacking the situation, and planned for every contingency, he is completely convinced that his way is the right way. That doesn't mean he won't listen. You can be sure he hears every word you say. But he will think about your input, and like the wheat and the chaff, he will use what he can and discard the rest.

LOVE

The Knight of Pentacles knows how to treat women, but is never a womanizer. He has a deep respect for women and wants them to feel good about who they are and what they can do. His sensitivity, along with his highly developed communication skills, helps him to relate to women. He is a gentle, understanding mate, and a lover who is more concerned with his partner's pleasure than with his own. He is the type of guy every woman who was ever treated with disrespect dreams about having for herself. The Knight has a deep love and respect for his mother and will confide in her about anything. He knows and trusts that her love for him is unconditional, and that nothing he tells her will change that love.

In his younger years, the Knight of Pentacles is unlucky in love and personal relationships. He is generally a loner when he is a teen, but once he moves on to college he falls in love, usually with the wrong person. She may be beautiful in body and put on a wonderful face in public, but underneath she might well be totally co-dependent, expecting him to do everything for her. Eventually, when he has had his fill of her behavior, they will go their separate ways, but his heart will indeed be broken, because when he loves, he loves completely. Also, his first relationship is generally contrary to his goals and ambitions, but he doesn't really learn that until the relationship is over.

The breakup with his first love is emotionally devastating, even years later. There is no way that he wants to repeat the error of his youth. His keen logic tells him that he needs someone more like himself; someone who can adapt to his goal-oriented lifestyle. He has no patience, time or desire to train a woman to live in his chosen way. The Knight of Pentacles will eventually have a second relationship. In his second relationship, he will find a woman like himself, and is careful not to repeat the mistakes he made the first time around. When he finally marries, it is only after he is certain that she will suit him in every possible way. The Knight won't marry until a bit later in life, sometimes in his late 20's but usually in his 30's. He feels he can't commit to a permanent relationship until his life is orderly and he is on the path to success.

The Queen of Pentacles is his best match. When they get together, they have a relationship that is the envy of all. She has the same attitudes and ethics he holds dear and they get along magnificently. Together, they make a truly perfect match.

The Queen of Swords is the worst match for the Knight. He sees her emotional reservation as selfish and unbelievable. Since she never seems to be happy, he perceives her as needy and whiny. He will avoid anyone who lives life with no common sense and no plan. Spontaneity, in the eyes of the Knight of Pentacles, is something best reserved for the bedroom.

HEALTH

The Knight of Pentacles is generally healthy, suffering only from self-induced problems. His drive to the goal brings on a fair amount of stress, and he suffers from the conditions that too much stress can cause. Anxiety, migraines, ulcers and high blood pressure are common in the Knight.

LEST WE FORGET

The Knight is a big collector of art and music. He is very inventive, and is always thinking of new ways to accomplish his goals. He is a true example of necessity being the mother of invention. He may play team sports in high school, but if he does, they are not the popular ones like football or basketball. He might end up on the soccer team or in individual sports like golf, tennis, track or swimming.

THE KING OF SWORDS

KING of SWORDS.

THE BASICS:

♠ Also known as: The King of Spades
♠ Sign: Eagle
♠ Flower: Kniphofia
♠ Gemstone: Onyx
♠ Characteristics: Authoritative, commanding presence, self-assured, very decisive
♠ Best Relationships: Queen of Swords, any of the Pentacle family
♠ Watchwords: "I make the rules"
♠ Manifestations of the spirit world: Electrical in nature, lights flickering

GENERAL

The Eagle is strong, fearless and independent, the epitome of the King of Swords, who does nothing less than to live life on his own terms. Like most other Sword people, the King is highly intelligent and sometimes seems abrupt. He is not generally viewed as a warm, kind and sweet individual. He is more often seen as no-nonsense, cut and dried, black and white in his opinions and somewhat rigid as a personality. He is a rule person. He is comfortable with the rules, he follows the rules and he expects others to follow them as well.

The King of Swords is most often found in a position of power in the community. He is the high-priced lawyer, the judge, the probation officer, the policeman, the government official or politician. He could also be a member of the church hierarchy, the upper echelon medical community, or even a General or other ranking military officer. The King of Swords wants and needs to have authority and control over as much of his environment as possible, be that work or community. A definite power monger, the King craves the respect of others and uses his power to shape his life and the lives of those around him.

PERSONALITY

Quite frankly, the King of Swords is best suited to rule the world. He is an analytical thinker, spends an inordinate amount of time making plans for attaining his goals and he has options for all the contingencies. He is an exceptional strategist, which is why he fits so well in the role of General or other commanding officer. The King knows where he is heading and what direction the things in his life are taking. He is always happiest when he is leading, and he is the type of person that people crave as a leader.

His presence is extremely authoritative, and people find comfort in the fact that such an able-bodied person is out front. It gives them the feeling that things will turn out for the best. But even while being authoritative, the King of Swords is still a people person. He can and will talk to anyone. He is never shy about speaking or expressing his opinion, but he never does it in a pushy manner, just in that quiet, powerful manner characteristic of successful men.

The King is innovative and creative in his work. He loves the challenge of planning strategy and watching the outcome. He likes to see a plan come together with the results he has in mind. But while he is that creative, authoritative leader at work, he is a totally different person with his family. He comes across as the head of the household. However, his personality is such that what he wants most for himself: success and power, he wants equally for his loved ones. He is not one to manipulate the people he loves, but he will provide them with every possible opportunity to achieve their own personal goals. He wants his loved ones to be individuals and to make the absolute most of the talents they have been given.

He is well aware of the differences between individuals and teams. He has no qualms about manipulating the soldiers on a battlefield to affect the outcome, but with family he acts as the ultimate support person, not as the all-knowing dictator. He is highly intelligent and respects the intelligence of his loved ones and prefers to nudge rather than push them forward in what they wish to do.

The King of Swords believes in letting his loved ones discover their own ways to happiness and success. He is never an enabler, believing that they learn even more from their failures than their successes. If his spouse or children want to do something he is wary of, he may warn them, but he will say go ahead and do it, see where it leads. He will support change and improvement 100%. If his spouse hates her job, and she needs four years off to get a degree in something totally different, he is all for it. If that means he helps with the kids while his wife is back in school, he will do so enthusiastically and without complaint. He is the type of man you could never imagine changing diapers, but one who does so with ease, almost by second nature, if he is helping out while his spouse is busy with self-improvements.

He improves himself and learns daily and wants to see her do the same. He is not nearly as interested in having common experiences with his spouse as he is in watching her achieve greatly in something, even if he has no interest in it at all. Anything she wants to do that involves growth and expansion as an individual, he will support. His backing of loved ones moving ahead in life is complete, physically, emotionally and financially.

The King of Swords is a very well spoken man. He rarely curses or uses foul language in front of anyone, and then only does so around his family or closest of friends. He is completely self-aware. He cares about the impression he makes on others, and is aware of the looks he gets and the things that are said about him. The King needs to be authoritative, and he knows that it is essential to look and act the part. To pull off the total authoritarian persona, it is necessary to be pulled together physically, emotionally and financially. You may notice that he has a tendency to use big words. He does not use them to be condescending, but to compliment the authoritative persona. It is possible that in doing so, he may be construed as being uppity, and at times he can be just that. The King is not used to being wrong about anything and can be a bit obnoxious in expressing his opinions.

EMPLOYMENT

As stated above, the King of Swords is most often found in the power positions. He is very suited for life in the legal realm because of his love for and adherence to the rules. He makes an excellent judge, meting out just sentences that fit the crimes. But his love for the rules often has him in related positions, such as lawyer, probation officer or policeman. He is always the best at what he chooses, so he is the one with all the awards on the wall over his desk, such as officer of year, heroism under fire, etc.

He is also found in high-ranking political or government

positions. He is likely to be the mayor or councilman, the city planner (because he loves order and strategy) or any other position that makes him an authoritative presence. But again, he is a good government official, not a crook. He plays by the rules and expects everyone else to do the same.

Similar to the policeman with all those awards, the King of Swords is also likely to be in a high-ranking military position. He is a leader of men and a strategic thinker, at the front lines directing troops, and in the war room working on the best possible plan of attack. But he is never looked on by his troops as a dictator, only a fair, just and intelligent leader who won't let them down in the thick of battle.

He could also be found in the church hierarchy, as an elder, a bishop or higher. When he chooses medicine, the King of Swords is generally at the top, as a department head, chief of staff or leading neurosurgeon. Regardless of the position, the King of Swords is seen as the ultimate authority in whatever profession he chooses.

APPEARANCE

Part of the persona of authoritative figures drives the King of Swords to be meticulous in his appearance. He is very neat in his home and of his person. He is the guy with creases in his jeans, never wrinkled even while doing physical labor. He wants to be seen as pristine, but he isn't obnoxious about his appearance. He buys good clothing and shoes, but not outrageously priced. He won't pay more than it's worth, but he will pay top dollar if he gets value for his money. He never has a hair out of place and always looks freshly showered and groomed. The King always stands out in the crowd. He doesn't smoke or use drugs because that would be against the rules and not socially correct. And he will only drink socially in a very limited fashion.

MONEY

The King of Swords is very good with money. He is not a greedy person and does not earn money for the sake of acquiring wealth. He views money as a necessity that is required for his own security and the financial well being of his family. He is not cheap, but he is frugal in that his money will be in safe, income-producing investments. He is a conservative investor and watches his money carefully. He needs to be in control of his financial universe, but he doesn't buy anything that is poorly made in order to save a dollar. Value for the money spent and solid, secure investments are his focus.

EMOTIONS

He is ambitious, reliable and often a driven man. The King is not afraid of people and not afraid to talk to anyone. He is very self-assured with only hints of insecurity. The King of Swords can give a speech in front of thousands and not think a thing about it. He rides an emotional high when all the eyes are on him and each person is hanging on his every utterance. He's not an actor, though he is performing when he gets up in front of people. He puts forth only himself, but in a better, more precise and clear way than if he is casually talking to a person one-on-one.

He may have had a difficult childhood, and he often has problems communicating his deepest feelings. When he can't communicate how he truly feels, the frustration may cause him to lose control, have a fit of temper, yell and get angry. In doing so, the King will develop ambivalent feelings toward himself. He wants and needs to be in control, and he wants others to perceive him as a quiet but powerful force, a steel structure that never sways under the buffeting winds of life. Only careful diligence on his part will prevent him from losing it to the point of being verbally abusive. And when he has difficulty communicating his feelings, others may be totally confused about where he is coming from and where he is going.

A very small hint of insecurity makes him love to be the

very best at everything he does, and he has a need to be recognized for his accomplishments. His ego needs occasional to regular stroking to keep him at his best.

LOVE

The King of Swords is very socially adept and always the perfect host. But to ever really become emotionally involved with him, a person has to be very intelligent and see past the power persona to the person in his soul. The King may become involved and marry early on, but generally will recognize it as a mistake and take steps to rectify the situation. Eventually, as he matures, he will take a very long time, however long it takes, to pick a partner who will suit him for life. He wants and needs someone intelligent enough to communicate with him on his level. But he also wants a woman who is self-assured and self-sufficient with interests that are separate and distinct from his own. The King of Swords will avoid clingy people, especially clingy women. The King has no time to waste on anyone who can't handle his or her own personal problems or life. He has no time to coddle, enable or waste solving someone else's problems when he is busy being powerful.

HEALTH

You may find the King of Swords working out at the local gym. He always takes good care of himself and his body and rarely, if ever, contracts any illnesses. Because he likes to be the best at the things he does, he excels at singular sports. He doesn't care to compete against others and is normally happy to best his own times and records, content in knowing he is improving himself in the effort. To that end, he will participate in sports such as archery, shooting, tennis, golf, handball, swimming or any other individual sport. The most frequent health complaints for the King of Swords are muscular aches and strains and intermittent back pain, usually from working out and pushing himself beyond the limit of his endurance.

LEST WE FORGET

The King of Swords loves the good things in life as they promote his powerful and authoritative persona. He drives a status car, wears well-cut clothing and buys only distinctive goods. He loves to dance and is very accomplished for a non-professional, but as in sports, it is an individual achievement. In his practical sort of way he is most likely to give gifts that will further the power and ambition of the recipient. Don't be surprised to receive stocks, bonds, certificates of deposit or the best in sports equipment as a gift from this King.

Socially, the King of Swords cares about his community and will involve himself in political agendas even if he has no personal political aspirations. If he aspires to politics, he has no problem attaining votes. He stands out in the crowd and people are drawn to him because he exudes an air of authority and stability that is so important to the masses. If he wants to run for mayor or governor or city council, he is most likely a shoo-in.

He always gives sound, well thought out advice. You can absolutely trust that he will give you accurate true information. The King of Swords is never afraid to make waves or take a stand, however unpopular. When the King is right, he's right. He has the power and authority to pull enough strings, when necessary, to accomplish his goals. He is not above manipulating a situation to make things come out in a fashion he deems is right.

The King expects all of his family members to be upstanding, and he has absolutely no tolerance for people who are blessed with opportunity that do not use it. He wants his children to use all of their talent. He is not one of those that will do a kid's homework, but he will give his child every opportunity and every tool necessary to achieve his or her goals.

The King of Swords is surprisingly sympathetic toward the handicapped, especially children. He is right there in the thick of things, running or supporting events like the Special Olympics for physically and mentally challenged children. And he avidly supports any cause for the handicapped, even going to bat for them politically if necessary. But he does not consider handicaps as excuses for poor performance. For example, if his child had Down's Syndrome, the child would not be coddled. He or she would be trained and educated to function at the highest possible level. The King of Swords believes deeply that everyone, no matter how limited in ability, should be given the opportunity to make the most of his or her capabilities. He believes that Army slogan "Be all that you can be" should apply to every human being across the board.

Not overly religious, the King of Swords is more a quiet spiritual type. He naturally follows prescribed church laws because he is totally about following rules and doing the right thing. He goes to church every week because he "should", because it is expected of him, and because it puts him out into the community in an acceptable social situation. You will often find him serving on church committees or on the local school board.

The King of Swords is not a particularly humorous person. And rowdy body or bathroom humor is totally out of character. Intellectual humor is more his speed; stuff you might find in publications for the well read, like The New Yorker, would be right up his alley.

He reads to learn, and he loves anything historical in nature. He may collect and restore antiques as a hobby, or even more specifically, he may collect books on battles (the strategist showing) or old maps and globes. In spite of his love of history, he likes gadgets and loves what high tech machines can do for him at work or at home.

Once the children are grown and out of the house, the King will take full advantage and spend a lot of quality time enjoying the company of his mate. When the King of Swords finally decides to retire, he trades his years of power mongering for more peaceful pursuits, such as quiet time with his spouse, puttering around in the garden, refinishing antiques, playing with the grandchildren or enjoying a scenic drive to the Grand Canyon. In essence, he graduates from power to peaceful and natural when he reaches his retirement years.

THE QUEEN OF SWORDS

QUEEN of SWORDS.

THE BASICS:

- ♠ Also known as: The Queen of Spades
- ♠ Sign: A Winter Forest
- ♠ Flower: Crocus
- ♠ Gemstone: Amethyst
- ♠ Characteristics: Intelligent, dutiful, judgmental
- ♠ Best Relationships: King of Cups, King of Swords, all Children of the Tarot
- ♠ Watchwords: "I follow the rules."
- ♠ Manifestations of the spirit world: Electrical in nature, lights flickering

GENERAL

Like a forest in winter, beautiful, sparkling and still, the Queen of Swords projects an air of cool composure. Yet, underneath that shimmering, snowflake and ice exterior, the Queen is a delicate spring flower, just waiting for Mother Nature to remove the obstacles that prevent her from emerging and unfolding to the world.

PERSONALITY

The Queen of Swords was most often one child in a large family, or she was born into a family with parents who were exceptionally busy taking care of the day-to-day matters of life. It's not that the Queen was neglected, but with so many other people and things competing for her parents' time, she quickly learned that she needed to make a concerted effort to be noticed. While growing up, her moments of glory were few and far between. That lack of praise fueled her lifelong struggle for recognition. The quest for attention makes her the overachiever in a family of hardworking, but otherwise unremarkable siblings.

She holds herself apart from others throughout her life, even, to a degree, from her husband and children. Often she finds herself outside of the intimate circle of living that the rest of her extended family experiences. Although she is a dutiful daughter, and manages her requisite family obligations with grace and ease, her life seems to take a different path than that of her siblings. Her drive to achieve and be acknowledged often impels her to move away from her origins, both physically and emotionally.

The Queen of Swords limits her true relationships to her husband and children, and she finds it difficult to develop close relationships outside of this limited group. She commands great respect in the workplace because of her intelligence; she is a true intellectual. However, like many intellectual people, she has a somewhat skewed view of others. It is sometimes difficult for her to understand why other people disagree with her judgement or question her expertise, both at home and at work. She is a font of

71

irrefutable knowledge, but makes no allowance for the fact that not everyone thinks or feels the same way she does. Unfortunately, this may cause people to perceive her as arrogant and controlling. While this is true to some extent, she truly doesn't understand that there are times when her thinking may be flawed. The Queen of Swords has researched and studied the topic; therefore, she must be right, at least in her own mind. Her intentions are good, and yet when people don't listen to her or take her advice, it appears that they don't appreciate her knowledge or accomplishments.

The Queen faces many challenges, both personal and professional, as she journeys the path of life. Even though she possesses all the right attributes, such as near genius intelligence and physical attractiveness, she often faces problems that are the result of other people's actions. The Queen learns quickly that the way things should be, and the way things really are, can be vastly different, almost to the point of opposition. Even so, she is still convinced that her way is the best way.

EMPLOYMENT

Because of her extraordinary intelligence, the Queen of Swords excels at complicated tasks. If there is research to be done, or if decisions requiring knowledge of all the facts need to be made, the Queen of Swords is the one to call. She always executes at her absolute best, whether the task is performing open-heart surgery, writing a novel or arranging flowers.

She is superb in any medical career. The Queen possesses the ability to accurately assess and diagnose problems and to suggest a course of action that makes the most sense, all while remaining detached enough to do what is necessary without any personal emotional involvement.

The Queen makes a top-notch administrator; she is no nonsense and all business, and would never allow anything or anyone in her charge to draw criticism. She insists on superior performance from anyone she employs. The Queen also makes an excellent teacher. Although she is not the really cool English teacher you had in high school, she is likely to be the one who taught you the most. Though you might not expect it, the Queen of Swords likes to take on the responsibilities for some of life's seemingly more frivolous activities. She is often the parent in charge of her daughter's Brownie Troop, head of the steering committee for beautifying her hometown, or stomping for signatures on a petition. If there is a good cause in need of a leader, the Queen of Swords is often the enthusiastic volunteer.

APPEARANCE

Always appearing younger than her chronological age, the Queen of Swords takes very good care of herself. She is one of those fortunate women who doesn't have to spend hours on her upkeep and always looks great. She loves beautiful clothing, jewelry and accessories, and always looks her best if she ventures out of the house. To that end, she buys the finest quality products at the lowest possible prices. She knows how to find the best sales. Since her clothing is always the best she can purchase, it lasts for many years. She won't throw it away because she knows that the cycle of styles will very likely repeat. She will always be ready to wear it again. Blessed with young skin and good genes, the Queen of Swords has no need of expensive cosmetics or plastic surgery to look her stunningly beautiful best.

MONEY

Never frivolous with her money, the Queen of Swords will always shop for the best deals. She is the woman with ten cases of toilet paper in her linen closet because she saw a good sale, had a good coupon, and planned to buy on double-coupon day, effectively getting the product for next to nothing. She is definitely a coupon cutter, very frugal in all of her spending. Although she will spend money on herself for luxuries such as travel, she is cautiously aware of every penny. She has money put away for a rainy day, and her savings accounts are always full and in good order. It is difficult for her to understand people whose spending habits indicate they are not worried about money. And though she buys in quantity on sale, she views as ridiculous having too much of an item that is not a normally purchased necessity.

When she is a young woman, and her husband is not able to make as much income as she deems necessary, she will stretch every dollar to make ends meet, rather than berate him for not providing. It doesn't matter if they eat cheaper cuts of meat, or if she has to sew clothes for the kids. She can cook and sew with the best of them, and doing so is preferable to making her husband feel inadequate.

The Queen of Swords is very community minded, but she may feel a bit wanting financially when faced with people who obviously have more money than she does. Although she will socialize with the Country Club set to a degree in doing her community work, she would not become involved with them on a personal level. Memberships in such organizations are much too costly, and though she may have the same sort of financial assets, she disdains wasting those assets on something she feels is excessive. The older she gets, the tighter her fist becomes, and she holds onto her money in an almost miserly fashion.

EMOTIONS

Emotionally, the Queen of Swords is an enigma. She can be very difficult to understand. On one hand she requires adulation from all around her, but at the same time, she can be almost uncomfortable with praise. The Queen lets her childhood rule her and is many times unable to convince herself that everything she does will not be subjected to scrutiny or criticism. She wants and expects extreme praise but anticipates reproach.

Sarcastic humor and teasing comments do not sit well with the Queen of Swords. She has no understanding of people who don't take themselves seriously, because she always takes herself seriously and would never think to tease others. The Queen has a rather fragile ego, so it is best to agree with her and not argue. Sometimes going along with her just makes your life simpler all the way around.

If she feels she has been treated with disrespect, she will sever ties with the person who dared to do so. The Queen is a passionate woman, and if she feels wronged it is not in her nature to forgive easily, especially if she perceives that wrong as a direct attack on her person.

She does, however, care deeply about how others view her, her actions and those of her family. Everyone and everything around her must be the epitome of propriety. She encourages her children to be "someone" and to make something good of their lives. However, the someone or something they choose to be or do better be on her list of approval. How they succeed, and how others view them, is a reflection on her. If and when they don't live up to her standards and expectations, she is sorely disappointed. If her children do not live up to her ideals of success, she will withdraw from their lives.

The Queen of Swords is often a lonely woman. This could be due to widowhood, divorce or design. It is often easier for her to live by herself than to battle the forces involved in establishing another relationship, at least on an emotional level. She finds contentment in busying herself with projects that benefit her community, actively seeking good causes she can spearhead and throwing her energies into leading the volunteers. Along with her small circle of friends, she engages in high-minded pursuits such as book clubs, bridge or traveling, most often to landmarks and historic places.

Responsibilities weigh heavy on her shoulders, and she finds that avoiding interaction with other people on an intimate level lessens her burdens. The Queen of Swords is at her best when she can successfully sway people to her way of thinking, and if that means that she gets to display her skills in the process, all the better.

LOVE

The Queen of Swords really has only one true love. She is happiest when she finds that love and is partnered with him for life. When the Queen finds her perfect partner, she understands the workings of his mind, and he understands hers as well. Her best mate is the King of Cups, whose philosophical nature is well suited to her enigmatic lifestyle. He seems to understand, better than most, what she is thinking and why she is acting in a particular way. She is an excellent caretaker of her spouse. The Queen will serve him only the healthiest of meals, and she is very attentive to all his health issues and his career.

She is often more concerned with his feelings and welfare than with her own, and this is an extreme departure from her normal demeanor! Widowhood hurts her more deeply, and the hurt stays with her much longer, than most women. She depends on her partner to intuit her needs and moods, and if this is taken away, she retreats into herself looking for that which is lost.

It is rare for the Queen of Swords to have the strength to begin a new relationship, especially if she is older. Some younger Queens who are widowed or divorced may remarry, but, even when young, most of these Queens will choose the solitary path. Choosing to be alone often eliminates the need to begin again and prove themselves to new partners.

The Queen of Swords will often depend on her children to pick up the tattered remains of her personal life. This is, of course, not the easiest thing for her children to deal with, but the Queen expects it, and so it is done. She is the mother and grandmother, and in her mind they owe her respect due to her age and station.

The children of the Queen of Swords are always independent and self-aware. The Queen expects extraordinary obedience from her children and can be unrelenting in her demands that they "do it right". Generally she does well with the children when they are very young, because they respond to every thing she does for them. However, as they get older, the kids become tired of building their world around her, and they lose interest. Eventually, most of her children exert their independence, and they strike out on their own at a very young age. They will usually manage to become successful, if not to please their mother, then as a personal challenge. Her best friend relationships are with Queens and Kings of Wands and other Queens of Swords with whom she feels great kinship.

HEALTH

The Queen of Swords is usually blessed with good health. She seldom gets even a common cold and is not usually on any type of medication. Sometimes she lives into very old age, 80 or more years, rarely taking even an aspirin. When she does suffer the occasional ailment, it will normally resolve itself, without so much as a trip to the doctor's office.

On the other hand, she may suffer from mental distress and disorders such as sporadic depression and, from time to time, the Queen shows a definite tendency toward narcissism. But her narcissistic bent is usually what keeps her focused on her own well being. The Queen of Swords is the most likely Queen to be able to take care of herself over the long term; not needing assisted living or nursing care until she is well beyond 80 years of age.

LEST WE FORGET

The Queen of Swords is highly adept with words and very well informed. She is an excellent Scrabble partner or teammate in Trivial Pursuit. The Queen has very broad interests, studying each one intently so that she is as learned as she can be in a particular subject. Dancing is one of her favorite activities, and she is often accomplished as a ballroom dancer. She also enjoys solitary pleasures such as flower gardening or reading. Always trying her hand at new things, she will have an interesting and eventful life, filled with wonder and many rich textures. She will never look back at her life with regret over things she never tried or things she left undone.

The Queen of Swords is very involved in organized religion. She attends services at the church of her choice faithfully and regularly, and fulfills all the religious duties of her faith. Actively involved, she teaches religion classes or runs the Sunday school. Her priest or minister knows her well, and knows she can always be called on to help out, even at the last minute.

She is also an excellent hostess. She doesn't throw large parties, but she will pull out all the stops if she has her bridge partners over for the afternoon. Pristine table cloth and napkins, a beautifully laid table and excellent edibles will always be waiting for her guests, when they arrive.

THE KNIGHT OF SWORDS

KNIGHT of SWORDS .

THE BASICS:

- ♠ Also known as: The Jack of Spades
- ♠ Sign: Lightening
- ♠ Flower: Oriental Poppy
- ♠ Gemstone: Moonstone
- ♠ Characteristics: Curious, adventurous, rushes through life
- ♠ Best Relationships: Queen of Wands, Knight of Pentacles
- ♠ Watchwords: "I bend the rules."
- ♠ Manifestations of the spirit world: Electrical in nature, lights flickering

GENERAL

Who can say that they are not fascinated by or even a bit fearful of lightning? The speed, the power, the beauty of nature's fit of temper is sobering yet awesome. You realize the danger, but you can't help watching with a morbid curiosity. Will it strike close to home? The Knight of Swords is like a bolt of lightning. He travels through life quickly, always striking a spark of energy with a hint of danger as he passes by. The Knight is a man known for his daredevil antics.

He is thrust into the spotlight at a very young age, and people look to him for excitement and entertainment. Both a performer and an individual achiever, there are no small deeds where the Knight is concerned. He is all or nothing. If he runs, he runs the farthest; if he jumps, he jumps the highest. If he drives, he drives the fastest. There are no half-measures for a Knight of Swords. He lives life to the fullest and savors all life has to offer. Greatness is not something he seeks, but he achieves fame through becoming the best at the things he loves to do. Causing a bit of a stir wherever he goes, he doesn't quite understand what the big deal is to other people, and his feelings about his fame are ambivalent.

The Knight thinks of himself as a regular guy, and, in a way, he is. His demeanor is friendly, outgoing, neighborly, and not the least bit pretentious, even though he surely has reason to be. The Knight of Swords becomes highly accomplished in everything he endeavors. He quietly works at it until he becomes the best and is then suddenly thrust into the limelight as an expert in the activity of his choice.

The Knight of Swords loves excitement and gets high on the adrenaline rush. Searching for that rush generally drives him into the extreme sports world. There he can constantly sate his need for thrills and has unlimited opportunities to excel on an individual level in an ever-growing variety of events. Motocross racing, flying stunt planes, high-speed boat racing and driving Indy cars are all activities that would capture his fancy. Most any sport that involves going like a bat-out-of-hell with significant risk to life and limb is right up his alley.

When he is not living life on the edge, he is involved in the high-tech world. Always looking for ways to put new technology to use in his activities, he may have a job that focuses on whatever technology has the potential to allow him to go faster, farther and higher. Regardless of the career he chooses; it will never be a boring one. He needs to be on the cutting edge; otherwise he might miss something.

The Knight of Swords is not impressed with himself, and he is never one to seek fame. He thinks the things he does are normal, fun, guy-things to do, and he doesn't understand why anyone else makes a big deal out of what he does. Usually he just wonders why THEY aren't doing these things too! Whether or not he impresses anyone else is completely immaterial. He does what he does because he craves action and is an adrenaline junkie.

PERSONALITY

The remark you will most often hear about the Knight of Swords is that he is a "sweetheart." Fame and fortune have no effect on his demeanor, and no matter how popular he becomes, he never forgets his family or his friends. He is a normal guy who just happens to be famous, rather than a famous guy who has forgotten how to be normal. He never puts on airs. Generous to a fault, the Knight is often the one doing a good deed, donating to a good cause or performing at a benefit. The Knight of Swords will always reach out to the less fortunate, no matter how famous he becomes. He will never forget those who helped him along the way, treating them all with deference and sincere, heartfelt gratitude.

The light of his presence is the confidence and kindness he exudes. People feel special and important when they are with

82

him, because he has a way of communicating that they are important to him. Co-workers always feel privileged to work with him, as he emanates a successful and harmonious aura. When given a compliment, the Knight of Swords will quietly say "Thanks", but becomes a bit shy and awkward in the process. He is most likely to achieve widely known status and fame, but he is the least likely of the Knights to become egotistical.

The goals he sets are, first and foremost, challenges meant to better himself. He has no desire to compete against anyone, and if the goal he sets for himself just happens to be a new world record, well, that's okay with him. But he won't do it just to say, "I set a new record"; he does it because he is seeking excitement, adrenaline rush and self-fulfillment.

The Knight of Swords really loves his toys. He will have the best available sports equipment and transportation (motorcycles, ATV's, etc.). But he also owns the latest sound system (in his home and his car), a state-of-the-art computer and a laptop to keep in touch on the road. He loves expensive high-performing "things" and will work hard to get them. But he is generous with those "things" as well, and thinks nothing of lending them to friends and family.

When the Knight of Swords considers you among the people he loves, he just can't do enough for you. He will do anything you ask of him and is an incredibly approachable and sympathetic listener. Whether the trouble needs application of money, time, labor or any other type of fix, he is the first to jump in and lend a hand.

EMPLOYMENT

The Knight of Swords is always working in careers where there are toys to play with and challenges to meet. He makes an excellent stuntman in the movies. He is the motocross star, the test pilot, the survivor of tragedy, and the daredevil.

He is the one who will "go where no man has gone before". When the first young pilot volunteers to set foot on Venus or

Mars, you can be certain he will be Knight of Swords. But he is also not too proud to play a support role as long as it is high tech, and one in which he is thinking of and planning new ways to have adventures unlike any experienced to date. Fast transportation is his first love, and he is likely to invent the first human transporter. He is always on the cutting edge. The Knight of Swords is undoubtedly the most exciting Knight in the Tarot Deck.

APPEARANCE

Appropriately dressed to suit his lifestyle, the Knight of Swords generally wears relaxed but stylish and trendy sports apparel. It is likely that a Knight of Swords invented the latest in running shoes, shorts and workout gear to facilitate his comfort while doing the things he loves to do. He suffers from a vanity of sorts. While he is not snobbish, he believes that how he dresses affects his performance, and he likes to be dressed in a manner that he feels has a positive affect. He doesn't put on any fronts, he shows up everywhere dressed as himself. And his manner of dress would never be mentioned or criticized.

The Knight of Swords is physically active, has a strong, lean, healthy body and walks about with an easy, attractive confidence. On the rare occasion (we're talking weddings and funerals at the very most) when he is expected to wear a suit, he looks like a model. But all he is thinking about is how fast he can ditch the duds and get back into REAL clothes. The Knight of Swords is generally clean cut. He isn't the type to sport faddish hairstyles, multiple body piercing or tattoos. He simply doesn't have time to be bothered with such expressions of social defiance. He is much too busy making sure he is up to date and ready to go. He always has a race to run and a goal to achieve!

MONEY

Financially speaking, the Knight of Swords feels relatively secure. It seems fairly effortless for him to find a way to earn money, especially since he knows he can earn money doing the things he really wants to do. The money, while important, is secondary to job satisfaction, but the money seems to follow him wherever he goes. He is rarely burdened with debt, because he prefers to live a life of freedom, and the only way to have real freedom is to never owe anyone; freedom from financial pressures is of utmost importance to him. The Knight won't squander his money on a lot of meaningless little things. He saves it for his new Harley or sports car.

EMOTIONS

The Knight of Swords is truly one who has no qualms about expressing his emotions. He will laugh, be concerned, be empathetic or cry as he feels at that moment, and he has no shame in doing so. Because of his reputation as a fearless thrill seeker, there are not too many who would ridicule him for making his feelings known. His love and concern for others is genuine, and he is a true friend in every sense of the word. Of all the Knights in the Tarot, the Knight of Swords is the most emotionally balanced.

LOVE

Not one to marry early on, the Knight of Swords is very slow to commit. He needs to get the thrill seeking out of his system before he can concentrate on a permanent relationship. He wants and needs to get it right, and usually has too much going on in his life to give a relationship all he's got. But when he is ready, he will put his entire being into the relationship. When he loves, he loves deeply; when he commits, he commits completely. It is very likely he will reach his late 20's or early 30's before even considering forming a permanent or even a long-lasting relationship.

When the Knight of Swords finally settles down to family life, he becomes totally family-oriented. He won't give up his toys; he will just take the wife and kids along on the dirt bikes and ATV's and make his love of those sports into fun family outings. Don't be surprised to see him riding with a 2 or 3 year old right in front of him on the saddle!

The Knight of Swords will wisely choose a supportive partner. He knows he will never retire completely from a life of action activities, so he needs a woman who is understanding, approving, and never discourages him from taking his forays into adventure.

HEALTH

The Knight of Swords is generally healthy. Most every doctor visit is for injuries sustained while pursuing his active lifestyle. Fractures, broken bones and pulled muscles are among his usual complaints.

LEST WE FORGET

The Knight is an ardent lover with lots of sex appeal. Although he is flattered by the attention, he thinks it ridiculous that he could be a heartthrob with adoring female fans. He is a seasoned traveler. He can set down roots and get to know the locals any place he ends up, no matter how temporary his stay. When he leaves a place he leaves devoted friends behind. But he never forgets those devoted friends and always stays in touch, either with a postcard, a phone call or a quick e-mail. The Knight is a very thoughtful gift giver. He doesn't just buy something and wrap it up like many men do. He puts thought behind a gift, and every gift he gives has meaning to the recipient.

Especially good with kids, the Knight always enjoys interacting with them. He finds them to be fresh and fun; after all, he is a kid at heart who never outgrew his love of fun and play. He never really grows up, his toys just cost more and need to be insured!

The Knight of Swords is spiritual in a personal sort of way. In his alone time, you might find him meditating, practicing yoga, repeating a mantra or studying Buddhist philosophy. He also believes that positive affirmation and envisioning can help him to achieve his goals.

THE KING OF WANDS

KING of WANDS

THE BASICS:

♣ Also known as: The King of Clubs
♣ Sign: The Great Stag of the Forest
♣ Flower: Chrysanthemum
♣ Gemstone: Tiger's Eye
♣ Characteristics: Reliable, responsible, honest
♣ Best Relationships: Queen of Cups, King of Wands,
   Queen of Wands
♣ Watchwords: "I will take care of it."
♣ Manifestations of the spirit world: Scents and odors
   announcing the presence of spirits

GENERAL

Powerful, silent and swift, the Great Stag of the Forest is the perfect archetype for the King of Wands. The epitome of stability and family values, there are few male types who are more reliable or as laid-back as this King is. He is the kind of man everyone wants to claim as a friend and every mother wants her daughter to marry. No, he's not a doctor, but he is an asset to any family unit. He takes all his roles, be it son, husband or father, very seriously. He is a blue-jeans type of guy, not afraid to work hard, and totally committed to his family.

The word "wuss" is not in his vocabulary. The King of Wands is a "real" man, 24 hours a day. He has his priorities in life set in concrete and sticks with them regardless of the changes in his environment or situation. He doesn't vacillate like other men do as they go from one situation to the next. He lives his life for family, and everything he does is for the betterment of those he holds most dear. He will do everything in his power to keep them safe and happy. They are his pride and joy, and it shows.

Multi-talented, multifaceted, there are not many tasks at which the King of Wands does not excel. From the standpoint of learning, the King is equally good as a student or as a teacher. He has a facility for guiding and leading impressionable youth; therefore, it is important that he not stray from his principles.

Those same principles will generally keep him faithful in a relationship. When he cares for someone, or loves a person deeply, he does so to distraction. By the same token, if he takes a disliking to someone, he will just ignore that person as though they don't exist, because for the King of Wands, they literally don't exist. He won't give such people the time of day. There's no middle of the road for the King of Wands. If he dislikes and ignores someone, take heed! He is a very accurate judge of character and sees hidden negative attributes that you and others may not recognize readily.

As with the Queen of Wands, the King naturally draws people into his arena. They innately perceive his warmth and strength, and they feel comfortable and safe in his company. Other men seek his friendship because he is totally genuine, a person who can be taken at face value with no fear of duplicity.

The King of Wands is amazingly wise with an almost genius level of common sense. He is the perfect person to go to if you need advice, and for goodness sake, if he gives you advice, follow it. He will always reveal the wisest course of action. And, as maddening as it can be, he's always right.

The King of Wands loves a good movie, and can sometimes be found glued to the American Movie Classics channel. He loves Westerns, where "men were men and sheep were scared". He is quite likely a John Wayne or Robert Mitchum fan, as they both had successful careers portraying typical King-of-Wands personalities in their movie characters. But the King is not a full-time couch potato; at least, he isn't in his younger days. The television is not a main attraction for him unless one of his classic movies is playing. It is merely a foul-weather pastime until he ages to the point of being less active. He loves the outdoors and leads a fairly active life until retirement age.

While he is still young and fit, he's just as happy to play with the kids in the backyard or to spend time participating in most any family activity or community function. And he is the type of father who participates in parent activities while his kids are in school or clubs; one of those parents who volunteers because he actually enjoys being involved in the kids' activities.

If there were such a phenomenon as an angel in disguise, it would be the King of Wands. It is likely that he has saved a life, or several lives, over the course of his present existence. He may even choose a career as a fireman, policeman or paramedic, where the opportunities to save lives abound. But regardless of career choice, the King is definitely the one to have around when things go south. He never panics in emergency situations, and with his genius level of common sense, he inevitably chooses the best course of action.

PERSONALITY

Some would call the King of Wands old-fashioned. He truly cherishes his intimates, but there are only a few who qualify for that type of relationship with the King. Those positions are reserved for his family and very few close friends.

Always selfless, the King of Wands is willing to lend a hand whenever needed, and he will go out of his way to do so. Whether his own project or that of someone else, he generally works quickly, but if he can't get it done today, he will methodically work on it by setting a certain amount of time aside each day for that purpose. Once he makes that plan, he follows it until the task is complete. This is a function of his tendency to be organized in his work efforts. He is generally neat while he works and cleans things up as he goes along. But be advised this does not apply to EVERY King of Wands. Occasionally you will find a slovenly King, but it is rare.

Even though he's always willing to help, all things considered, the King would rather be at home. He is emotionally attached to his domicile with a psychological bungie cord, only going so far before bouncing back to that which is familiar and comfortable. When his work and play are done for the day, you will find him in his favorite chair, remote in hand, and American Movie Classics or Discovery Channel on the tube.

The King of Wands is a traditional family man. A deep connection to Mother Earth, common in those of the Wands family, fosters his love of planting, harvesting and building. He is likely to build or garden on a massive scale, and sometimes grows and harvests much more than he can use. He values home and all things that signify home in his mind. As a result, he often collects antiques and family heirlooms, but not for his own financial betterment. He wants to leave those things as a legacy for his children, expecting them to put equal or greater value on those things that are important to him. He says they are an investment for their future, but in his heart he can't believe that they would sell such things for personal gain.

Not one to leave anything to the fates, the King of Wands always has a contingency plan. He is a true Boy Scout, always prepared. Though fair-minded, the King has a stubborn streak a mile wide once his mind is set on a particular issue. In spite of his mild-mannered, laid-back attitude, don't be fooled! Never hurt someone that the King of Wands loves and cherishes. Although he is not a violent personality, he will get his revenge. A firm believer in the theory that there is "more than one way to skin a cat," he will find a punishment suited to the crime that will not require physical contact. He will plan carefully, and he will bide his time awaiting the perfect opportunity. Justice will be forthcoming, that is a given. The justice is likely to be considerably painful, be it emotional, financial or just plain bad publicity. The King is not above causing that person to lose his or her employment or good reputation in the community. He firmly believes in the public's right to know!

Forget about the mundane details of daily living, the King of Wands doesn't know or care about things such as balancing the checkbook or taking care of the bills. He'd much rather just hand over his paycheck and let his capable mate take care of those particulars. The King is generally well mannered and respectful. He tries to avoid being judgmental and will give the benefit of the doubt to almost everyone, until, of course, they do something to prove they don't deserve his trust.

He owns at least one suit, but you aren't likely to see him wearing it unless he must attend a wedding or a funeral. The King of Wands is the height of casual. He prefers dressing for comfort, and jeans and tee shirts or flannel shirts comprise the larger share of his wardrobe. He often has favorites in his casual attire and will wear them until they are threadbare and beyond. If you throw one of his favorites into the trash, don't be surprised if he retrieves it! Trust me when I say the only way to keep him from continued wearing of such a favorite is to cut it into completely non-repairable, non-wearable shreds.

The King of Wands has a good, but rather dry, sense of

humor, loves to laugh, and prefers to keep things light.

EMPLOYMENT

If the King of Wands is your mate, you needn't ever worry about paying the rent. He is the quintessential provider. He works tirelessly to provide the essentials and more for his family, usually to the degree of being labeled a workaholic. The King is indeed a hardworking man and is usually, but not always, employed in a blue-collar trade job. He loves working with his hands and enjoys the freedom of not being tied to a desk. He would definitely not be happy occupying a "cube". The King finds adherence to rigid schedules rather loathsome, but he also understands and values on-time completion of projects, and will make a huge effort to get things done in a timely fashion.

The King of Wands would be an excellent teacher because of his overabundance of patience and his laid-back attitudes. He is blessed with the ability to pass his knowledge to others, young and old alike. Although he is not the first to jump up and volunteer to give a speech, his ability to communicate is far above the norm and he will do well if put in that position. He is admired for his ability to impart his wisdom, and he is sought after to take on the role of disseminating information to the public in a variety of venues. You may find him donning the education and speaking role as a teacher, a public servant, a little league coach or a Boy Scout leader.

APPEARANCE

A ruggedly handsome, fit guy, the King of Wands is not the type to sit around. His hard-working nature is the basis of his naturally strong, healthy look. And nature has left him fit to a degree. But be aware that once he ends his years of being highly active for any reason (retirement, injury, etc.) he will get out of shape very quickly and become an aging couch potato with a comfortably soft potbelly.

MONEY

The King of Wands both earns and spends money freely. He works hard for his money, but he likes to have fun too. He loves his toys, whether boats, tools, motorcycles, high-powered digital music equipment, computers or big screen TVs. But his free spending does not mean there's no fallback cash. Financial security is his first concern and he always has a back-up plan!

EMOTIONS

The mate of any King of Wands will tell you that her significant other has an abundance of compassion for people, especially those in dire financial straits through no fault of their own. He is highly aware of world events, and his heart bleeds for the poor and suffering, the sick and the displaced. Starvation, rampant illness and war wound him deeply regardless of where on the globe they occur.

But don't be fooled by that compassion. He has no patience or understanding for those who are too lazy or unwilling to even try to change their situations. He is kind of like God in the respect that he is willing to help those who are trying to help themselves.

Profoundly spiritual by nature, the King of Wands holds an unquestioning belief in God and trusts that God won't let him down. He also knows that what goes around comes around, although he has no problem in helping it "come around" when someone he loves has been hurt or wronged.

In spite of the difficulty he sometimes has in expressing his feelings, the King always wants what is best for his kids and openly shows affection for them. By the same token, his kids recognize that affection and return it in kind. In many cases, his children are comfortable enough with their family situation to live at home until marriage or a job opportunity lures them away. And although the King has no qualms about them living at home until they are ready to leave, he would never stop them if they wished to go.

The King of Wands wants to be a good father to his

children. But he also wants his kids to view him as a friend, and so takes great pains in trying to understand them. His protective nature impels him to be the friend his kids come to first when they have a problem or they need to talk. In this way, he can continue to exert a nurturing and protective influence over them, not to stifle, but to guide.

Getting older does not appeal to the King of Wands, and the realization that the march of time cannot be stopped sometimes results in periods of withdrawal, reclusiveness or negativity.

LOVE

Although he's likely to marry at a fairly young age, the King of Wands is not really comfortable in a permanent relationship until he reaches his 30's. The King is a tactile and sensuous lover. He loves to hug and touch and cuddle and enjoys the art of giving pleasure to his mate.

The King is a considerate and loving husband and will always take care of his partner. He never tries to dominate her, however, and he always treats her as his equal. If his wife wishes to work, the King doesn't have any problem with that. If she wants to stay home, he won't object to that either. Most important decisions are made as a team, and even child rearing is done in agreement. The King of Wands will always love and admire his spouse for being an individual in her own right.

The best love match for the King is the lovely Queen of Cups. Her ethereal and somewhat mystic demeanor goes a long way in creating a balanced marital situation, offsetting the King's over abundance of realism and logic. The King of Wands has a really hard time relating to the Knight of Cups. His common sense and logic make it hard to accept the Knight's lifestyle of almost deliberate and total irresponsibility.

HEALTH

For the most part, the King is amazingly healthy. He may have a tendency, because of his consistent work habits, toward repetitive motion injuries such as carpal tunnel syndrome. He may also suffer from bad joints, torn cartilage and ligament problems, especially in his knees. And he may develop arthritis in those joints as the years pass by. High blood pressure could be a problem with this King, so he needs to get checked regularly. Because he looks and feels healthy 95% of the time, a high blood pressure condition could exist for quite a long while without being discovered. His overabundant compassion might sometimes causes anxiety attacks, some nervousness and insomnia, or simply disturbed sleep patterns.

LEST WE FORGET

You won't always need to do the cooking if the King of Wands is your mate. He may not be a gourmet chef, but the food he is confident to prepare will always be made superbly. He is so adept at cooking his "specialties", that anyone who samples them will request that he make those dishes for holidays and special occasions. Holidays are special for the King of Wands, and he loves preparing for them and enjoys the myths surrounding them. He is likely to carry on the traditions he has learned as an adult and wants to pass the importance of those traditions to his children.

Be aware that if you borrow one of the King's tools, you had best return it in pristine condition or you will never be allowed the borrowing privilege again. The King is fussy in caring for his "toys" because he's worked so hard to acquire them.

The King of Wands likes to gamble, and may enjoy a trip to Vegas or Atlantic City, but he is not a candidate for Gambler's Anonymous. He knows when to stop (ever practical) and he will only gamble for fun and to try to help the family out a bit. Since his main thrust in life is to provide for and protect his family, he will never gamble away the savings account. He will play the lottery, but he won't blow his paycheck in the process. He might buy a ticket or two every week, hoping he might get lucky.

The King of Wands likes animals, especially bigger dogs

that he can take out for a run in the woods or nearby vacant lot. Although he likes pets, he doesn't like the responsibilities of pet ownership, so don't be surprised if visits to the vet and pet clean-up tasks are delegated to others.

He likes music, within limits. He prefers ballads, folk and country, and other types of easy listening, but no acid rock or rap for this King. He detests the loud noise, screaming and pounding of those types of music. The King of Wands reads, but he is particular about his chosen material. He will generally stick to books and periodicals about things in which he is interested, such as gardening or sports. His driven mechanical side will keep him reading only fiction that is reality-based and technical, such as the works of Tom Clancy.

THE QUEEN OF WANDS

THE BASICS:

- ♣ Also known as: The Queen of Clubs
- ♣ Sign: The Majestic Oak Tree
- ♣ Flower: Sunflower
- ♣ Gemstone: Emerald
- ♣ Characteristics: Nurturing, healing, benevolent
- ♣ Best Relationships: Anyone
- ♣ Watchwords: "Please...let me help."
- ♣ Manifestations of the spirit world: Scents and odors announcing the presence of spirits

GENERAL

The Majestic Oak Tree stands strong and silent, like a safe harbor in the wild woods. Her branches and leaves offer refuge to animals and birds alike, and her shade provides protection from the hot rays of the sun. Like that mighty tree, the Queen of Wands stands as a beacon, peaceful and serene, a haven of comfort, guidance and healing to those around her. The equivalent of the Queen of Clubs in an ordinary deck, she is the nurturing significator of the Tarot. A font of caring, teaching, healing and protection; children and animals gravitate toward her and love her for they know, instinctively, that she will take them in and shield them from the bad things in their world. Unfortunately, some people think trees will always be there, and that one tree is much like the next. Sometimes the Queen of Wands is treated in a similar fashion: unnoticed, taken for granted, treated like a fixture.

PERSONALITY

The Queen of Wands is a natural-born nurturer and healer. Her soothing and healing personality helps keep the unsettled aspects of the world in a state of relative calm and equilibrium. As a member of the Wand family, the Queen of Wands is a born truth-sayer. She faithfully keeps your confidences, and when she counsels you, she always speaks the truth.

There is no better person to have as a friend than the Queen of Wands because of her unswerving loyalty. She is definitely not the fickle type and does not easily change her mind or her opinion of people. But she is not averse to change if all the evidence points to a change making sense. And sense is something she possesses in abundance. Everything the Queen does is well planned and completely thought through. She's always at ease with people, and she's very outspoken in a practical sort of way.

The Queen of Wands is rooted to the earth, bound to it by her love of nature. Her deep connection to nature is innate, simply because she is of nature herself. She loves spending time outdoors, whether playing with the kids, participating in a sport or just communing with the wide-open spaces, the plants and the animals. Each change of season is an event for the Queen of Wands. She loves watching earth's cycles as nature renews, matures, ends and renews yet again each passing year. Because she is always in tune with these cycles she is a natural gardener, knowing what to plant, when to plant and exactly when to harvest for the best results.

The Queen is also adept at using the products of nature. She is an excellent cook; a skill she comes by naturally, of course. A "seat-of-the-pants" cook, she makes entire feasts by just throwing ingredients together; no recipes required. Often, she has no idea how she manages to produce such delicious repasts, but no matter what she cooks, compliments on the superb tastes and flavors abound. You may see evidence of her "magic pot" when you are a guest in her home. The magic pot is bottomless, rather like the biblical baskets of loaves and fishes. If four people are expected to arrive for dinner, but eight people show up on her doorstep, her "magic pot" expands to meet the need. There is always enough to feed the crowd. No one ever goes away hungry from the dinner table of the Queen of Wands.

EMPLOYMENT

Determination is the cornerstone of the Queen's work philosophy. She can and she will succeed in whatever career she chooses. She thinks through her career options carefully, chooses the one she thinks will best suit her, then goes after that career with all the ferocity of mother lion on the Serengeti. This does not mean that she is ferocious at work. On the contrary, the Queen of Wands is calm and easy-going on the job but always works in an active, high-energy way. She is pleasant, quiet and efficient. Always working in the background, the Queen of Wands is that irreplaceable person who gets things done. It's not likely that anyone even notices what she does at work, unless, of course, she is not there to do it and things begin to fall apart. Then everyone notices. But co-workers have short memories. Once she returns to carry on, they go back to taking her for granted.

Caring more about working in a career that suits her than in having a "proper" woman's role, the Queen of Wands is often found in gender-bending jobs. She is just as likely to be an engineer as a nurse, a construction worker as a secretary. But her grounding in nature, and her nurturing and healing character, make her best suited for jobs in medicine, teaching, childcare and people services. Regardless of her chosen profession, the Queen of Wands always works harder than just about anyone, but that does not stop her from always being the first to lend a helping hand when needed. Looking for someone to head up that United Way Drive, to recruit Red Cross Blood Donors or to spearhead a food for the hungry campaign? The Queen of Wands is your best bet if you hope for a successful endeavor.

APPEARANCE

The Queen of Wands is a natural beauty. She is not necessarily beautiful in the sense that a model is beautiful, but rather in a slightly less feminine way. Amazonian, or perhaps handsome, would describe it best. She walks with a natural ease and gait, radiating good health, strength and confidence. She wears clothing well and is equally presentable in threadbare jeans and a pullover or the latest designer gown. She is not the type to spend hours mulling over what to wear to any particular function, or whether to wear sling-backs or loafers, because everything looks good on her. It is only on a very rare occasion that she would bother with putting on any make-up. Her natural radiance is incredibly attractive and infinitely more appealing than anything artificially applied. Other women are often envious of the Queen of Wands, because they just can't seem to duplicate the confidence and ease of motion that the Queen seems to manage effortlessly. They spend inordinate amounts of time and money trying to achieve a look and presence even remotely similar to the natural aura that is the signature mark of the Queen of Wands.

MONEY

The Queen of Wands is rather like that investment firm that makes money the "old-fashioned way". She knows the value of, and reward for, hard work, and she is not afraid to get her hands dirty in carrying out the duties of her employment. She works efficiently, and she works diligently, to make sure that she has the financial wherewithal to meet her obligations. As long as she is able-bodied, she will provide for her family to the best of her ability. Her bills will always be paid and her family will be sheltered and fed. Life with the Queen of Wands will always be a financially stable one, not necessarily one of wealth, but at the very least, secure.

EMOTIONS

In much the same way that she is taken for granted in the workplace, the Queen of Wands is often taken for granted by those in her personal life. She might as well have "martyr" tattooed on her forehead. She is incredibly trusting of others, almost to the point of naivete. More often than not, she gets used and stepped on as a result of that trust. A typical mother to all, she keeps doing and doing for everyone regardless of the fact that many "friends" and "relatives" never appreciate what she sacrificed to help them. Her strong emotional ties to loved ones fuel her innate sixth sense; she knows instinctively what they need, and she will go to great lengths and beyond to help them, even if they are terrible ingrates.

Because the Queen instantly gives her trust to almost anyone, people who manage to get close to her freely tell her lies and try to sell her one bill of goods after the next. In most close relationships, she instantly becomes a doormat, getting walked on regularly. But the Queen of Wand's doesn't seem to notice her doormat status, she's too busy taking care of everyone around her or working to make sure that her home and family are secure.

To say that her concern, love and caring for others can be a detriment to her own well being is an understatement. She is so concerned about everyone else, she often neglects her own needs. It is not unusual for a Queen of Wands to remarry the same man, or at the very least, allow him to move back in with her, even if the break-up was not amicable. She feels sorry for him and her need to help outweighs her common sense. But mothering and caring for others is her nature. She needs to take care of others in the same way she needs to breathe.

The Queen of Wands is very uncomfortable with the concept of death, especially the deaths of those close to her. The effects of a loved one's death may last months or years. In some cases, she may continue to visit the grave of a loved one annually, and often has difficulty coming to grips with a death that happened while she was young, such as losing a childhood friend or a grandparent. But although she's uneasy with death, you will always find her at the bedside of a loved one at the end. She simply has to be there because it is her calling to assist people in making the transition to the heavenly plane. Her presence has a tranquilizing effect on the dying. She is able to help them relax through the pain and find their way to the light. This is an extremely important function as many need to be calmed and reassured, and sometimes even given permission to move on, before they will allow themselves to go toward the light and pass over.

LOVE

The most compatible mate for the Queen of Wands is the King of Wands, the strong, quiet, dependable family man. He is the most likely to understand and tolerate her need to help others, and will continue to love her enduringly, long after other men would have given up in frustration and moved on.

But sometimes her drive to help people who have "needs" may compel her to become romantically involved with the King of Cups. This is not always a bad thing; at least from the standpoint that such a match feeds her need to nurture, although there are occasionally times when making such a match is not in her best interest. If a King of Cups is one with a total lack of emotional availability, the Queen might find the situation highly unsatisfactory and sometimes intolerable. This would not necessarily cause her to change her course, however, because the Queen of Wands thinks she can change and fix things. She always anticipates the needs of her mate and works hard to fill those needs, even if it is a life-long losing battle.

In the event that she finds herself involved with a person who absolutely does not return that love and caring, she may find the strength to remove herself from that situation, especially if she is still young. But many Queens of Wands spend their entire lives stuck with a using, selfish mate. Of all the Queens of the Tarot, the Queen of Wands is the most likely to be divorced, often multiple times.

Those ingrates who depend on her will go to great lengths to discourage the Queen of Wands from making any substantial changes in her work or lifestyle. She is responsible for the stability in their lives and they certainly don't want that to change. And they also wouldn't want to lose someone who would do anything for them. It would disturb the otherwise carefree flow of their lives; the carefree flow that would not exist but for the efforts of the Queen.

Because they all know of her inability to say "no" to their needs, mooching friends, greedy kids and countless organizations keep calling to ask her to give more time and resources to their causes. It is certainly not unusual for a Queen of Wands to be the only Girl Scout Leader whose kids have long since outgrown the organization and are all adults with lives of their own.

HEALTH

The Queen is actually a very healthy person, although you might not divine that from her demeanor. She loves low impact sports but hates formal exercise. She is likely to be found swimming or biking, but when it comes to sit-ups or stair climbing, you won't find her participating. Even though the Queen of Wands will expend enormous amounts of energy doing something she enjoys, she simply does not believe in exercise for the sake of sweating. It is actually a good thing that she shies away from high-impact activities, because she is likely to be afflicted with joint pain and arthritis in her later years from living such a high-energy life.

On the rare occasion that she does becomes sick, the Queen is likely to choose natural or homeopathic remedies over more conventional medicines. Her connection to the Earth is so strong that taking the natural route as treatment is the only viable choice, at least in her own mind.

Although the Queen of Wands will occasionally imbibe in a wee bit of alcohol for medicinal reasons, she is almost never one to be caught in a cycle of drug or alcohol abuse or addiction. Those stimulants hold no appeal for her. She gets all the "high" she craves from doing things for others and has no need for artificial stimuli.

The biggest health drawback for the Queen of Wands is actually her normally "good" health. Because she so rarely becomes ill, she has a tendency to shrug off aches and pains as minor irritations and inconveniences, and in doing so, can sometimes be blissfully ignorant of a serious health condition in the making. She habitually avoids doctor visits believing that whatever is bothering her at the moment is just an annoyance that will vanish as mysteriously as it arrived. The Queen needs to be vigilant and regular in getting routine physicals and gynecological examinations to catch any serious problem she might otherwise ignore until it is too late to obtain treatment.

LEST WE FORGET

The Queen of Wands has an extraordinary gift for interaction with kids and animals. Even if they can't communicate wants and needs adequately, she instinctively understands what is needed. She loves and understands them all equally well, whether they belong to her or to someone else. Children naturally gravitate to her because they can sense that she is safe and will keep them safe as well. Even injured wild creatures will allow a Queen of Wands to minister to them, because they sense that she is a part of the earth and will not harm them.

Being part of the earth, the Queen of Wands finds comfort and satisfaction in activities that reflect her origins. Because she needs to stay in touch with the earth and feel grounded, she is often an avid gardener and can frequently be found working the earth and planting a wide variety of flowers, herbs, vegetables and foliage. She is also quite likely to be an herbalist, either as a hobby or a calling. She understands the uses and abuses of herbals and is a natural at the art of matching the correct herb to the correct problem. She often has curious bottles and containers of strange herb substances on her shelves. Had the Queen lived 150 years ago, she would have been branded a witch for her herbal efforts. Because she is firmly grounded, and those of the spirit world find her to be a safe haven, she is the most likely to have medium-ship abilities.

As an earth-based creature, the Queen is highly in tune with her senses. She craves anything that heightens her awareness; an emotional piece of music, a sensual touch or a new exotic food. Her enjoyment of such things seems incredibly erotic to any interested onlookers, even though she may not be aware of the sexuality that her enjoyment of such things exudes.

Practicality is abundant in the earth-based Queen, but that does nothing to curb her creative impulses. She is highly prolific when it comes to arts and crafts, especially those that are involved with activities that keep her rooted to Mother Earth. She is forever arranging fresh flowers, making door wreaths and swags and other decorative arrangements. She is also likely to be hunched over a pottery wheel. She finds satisfaction and stress relief while keeping her hands in Mother Earth.

THE KNIGHT OF WANDS

KNIGHT of WANDS.

THE BASICS:

♣ Also known as: The Jack of Clubs
♣ Sign: Quiet Lake
♣ Flower: Marigold
♣ Gemstone: Lapis Lazuli
♣ Characteristics: Unassuming, hard-working, kind, loyal, quietly ambitious, justice-serving
♣ Best Relationships: Queen of Wands, Queen of Cups, Knight of Pentacles
♣ Watchwords: "Let me do that for you."
♣ Manifestations of the spirit world: Scents and odors announcing the presence of spirits

GENERAL

There are few places that are quieter, more serene, than a mountain lake, formed by some ancient volcano, still, cool and deep, unspoiled by human hands. The Knight of Wands is such a lake. He is calm, peaceful and serene--most of the time. But he is an enigma. He has two personalities. For if he perceives injustice, his ability to defend and protect bursts forth from that lake like an underlying dormant volcano suddenly awakened. Injustice arouses the sleeping giant. Remember that the surface of the quiet lake is just that--the surface. Much goes on under the surface, be it a quiet lake or the Knight of Wands.

The Knight is a very likeable guy, a good guy by most people's estimation. He is never pretentious. He always seems to be exactly what he appears to be, a good son, and a helpful brother. He is the grandson that visits his grandparents under the guise of social contact, but is really there to make sure everything is okay and to change those light bulbs Grandma can't reach. He's the attentive boyfriend who really does care more about his girl than he does about himself. And if he works for you, even if he crabs about his duties, he's the worker you can always count on to go the extra mile. He is consistently reliable, responsible and is always accountable for his actions. He won't lay the blame on anyone else. When you are with the Knight of Wands you will always feel very safe.

On one hand the Knight of Wands is best described as predictable. Surprises with him are few and far between. As long as the people he has to deal with are behaving in an uncomplicated, fair and moral way, he is perfectly mild mannered. On the other hand, beneath his calm exterior there lives a temper that is reserved solely for injustice. The Knight of Wands cannot stand to see anyone being treated unfairly. He will stand up to his employer if a co-worker is being berated in public. And if his father is being abusive or dishonest with his mother (whom he loves dearly), the Knight will give him a verbal shellacking. And woe is he who abuses a child, for the Knight will confront the offender, challenge him, and not let up until the offender is paying the legal price for his crimes. The Knight of Wands can be very stubborn and single minded in serving the cause of justice, and he will not back down until the situation has been diffused or rectified.

He can be incredibly unforgiving; especially if you have damaged the reputation of someone he loves or caused them physical harm or mental anguish. The Knight of Wands does not believe in playing games and has no tolerance for those who do. Honesty is very important to him and he values it in others above all else. Like most of the Wand people, he will take the high road, carefully traversing the web of lies and deceit that many people surround themselves with as a way of life.

He will like you unconditionally until you prove that you can't be trusted. Once that trust is lost, he will never trust you again, no matter what you do to try and make the situation right. And if you betray his trust in any way involving his mother, siblings or girlfriend, you can be absolutely certain he will never again give you even the time of day. Just remember, even though he appears gentle and methodical, like that quiet, mountain lake, beneath his calm surface lies a dormant volcano, ready to come back to life.

PERSONALITY

The Knight of Wands is very family and friend oriented. He hates discord and dislikes confrontation. But he will confront on matters of injustice. He wants everyone to be happy and doesn't like it much when things are discordant or tense. The Knight can be playful, and he interacts well with pets and children. He can play games at their level. Very cautious in choosing a life partner, he needs to know he can have complete and total trust in the person he chooses to be his mate. He tests her for quite some time before making a permanent commitment. He will work incredibly hard to provide for those he loves, and is unswerving in his loyalty to them.

EMPLOYMENT

In keeping with the traits of most Wand people, the Knight of Wands will take any job in an effort to achieve independence. He feels no work is demeaning, and will take whatever he can get in time of need with no qualms or shame whatsoever. He is a caretaker and a defender, so he is often found in jobs that make the most of his innate skills. Teaching, food services, maintenance and medical positions are all common choices for the Knight of Wands. He can also be commonly found working in the trades as a carpenter, plumber, electrician or doing any other construction-type labor. He is your trusted, local auto mechanic. And a darn good one at that.

If a Knight of Wands chooses to work in the trades, he is very likely to end up owning his own business. He is most often a sole proprietor because he wants it done right and he wants to do it his way. When he is the owner, all employees are treated justly. You will almost never find an ex-employee suing him for any reason. He has an incredibly strong work ethic, and you can be sure that what he does is done well. If it does not meet the demands of his customers, he will do it again and again, if need be, until they are satisfied.

APPEARANCE

When it comes to clothing, the Knight of Wands is as informal as they come. Sometimes he dresses comfortably to the point of looking a bit unkempt. The loose, relaxed look is his favorite because he hates clothing that restricts his movement, and he often buys things a size or two larger than he really needs! The Knight is a tee shirt and jeans guy when he is out on the town, and a definite sweats guy at home. He keeps his hair cut short or buzzed. And he doesn't really care if it is the most attractive look for him or not; short hair means less work on his own personal upkeep. He may have an occasional tattoo or pierced ear, but he never goes overboard, simply because he sees no point in inflicting pain on himself.

MONEY

The Knight of Wands works hard from an early age, usually securing his first paying job around the time he hits 14, and he is almost always that fresh-faced kid behind the counter at McDonalds or Burger King. His needs are few; he does not require expensive trappings. He does buy reasonably serviceable clothing, and may even do a little catalog shopping to acquire his wardrobe. Spending little on himself, he is an avid saver, sometimes with multiple savings accounts, 401K and long-term CDs. He will spend his money only on good causes, and he is more than willing to generously give money to anyone he feels genuinely needs and deserves his help.

EMOTIONS

The Knight is noticeably polite and much more genteel of manner than most people his age. He always inquires about how others are feeling, and he is genuinely concerned about their health and state of mind. He has an infinite capacity for compassion, sympathizing with people who are troubled, and he will listen to them patiently as they tell their tales of woe. He has boundless empathy for those afflicted with physical or medical problems; much more so than his peers. The Knight of Wands is tender hearted and is more likely than the rest of the Knights to say the right thing at the right moment. His understanding of people often surprises those around him who are confused at such wise, philosophical views in someone they perceive as just an ordinary guy.

LOVE

Extremely considerate of all females, the Knight of Wands would never be physically, verbally or emotionally abusive. He falls in love just once, generally early in life, and he will love that girl for his lifetime. If the girl he picks is the right one for him, the Knight will love and care for her without reservation. The Knight of Wands often comes from a family where the father or male authority figure is immature, critical and abusive. His lifetime of protecting and defending starts with standing up for his mother against abuse he sees in his own home. He learns to be the man of the house while still young, and those lessons in responsibility follow him through life. But he also learns to keep to himself any thoughts that bring down his father's verbal abuse and ridicule. This is the impetus for his strong, silent-type persona.

HEALTH

For all his wonderful qualities, the Knight of Wands has more than his share of over-indulgences and unhealthy habits. He is not likely to dabble in hard drugs, but does occasionally imbibe in the camaraderie of downing a few (or maybe too many) beers with his buddies. He loves good food and, unfortunately, has a tendency to live with yo-yo syndrome. While he is young, he maintains a decent weight only by the work of his brow. All that labor burns off the calories of his edible indiscretions. But it is not unusual for him to suffer from overweight when he gets a bit older and is not as physically active. Medically, he is also prone to hypertension and anxiety disorders. He sometimes suffers from depression because he oftentimes feels alone. He is compelled to go through life always giving to others, taking nothing for himself.

LEST WE FORGET

The Knight of Wands makes a great husband. If you marry him, you can be sure that he will always be faithful and never let you down. Kids and animals are just fine with him. He loves being with them and teaching them. His childlike, innocent sense of humor puts children at ease, and they are not stiff or standoffish around him as they are with other adults. The Knight is often a practical joker. He is never malicious, but he enjoys making people laugh and often will do so at his own expense.

Doggedly persistent, he will achieve the things that he feels are truly important to him, such as a college degree, a job he loves or a business of his own. Because he is the strong and silent type, it is very easy to underestimate his intelligence and his capabilities. But don't make that mistake! You could be in for one very large surprise, because this Knight's quiet-lake packaging often hides what lies beneath.

Another thing you should know is that you will never be lacking a decent meal with the Knight of Wands. He is an excellent cook, and in his search for a suitable career in a service position he may decide to be a chef. And as in all things, if cooking is his passion, he will be incredibly adept at the task.

CHILDREN OF THE TAROT

PAGE ᴏ̆ CUPS.

THE BASICS:

- ♥ Sign: Dove
- ♥ Flower: Baby's Breath
- ♥ Gemstone: Quartz crystal
- ♥ Characteristics: Wise beyond years, dreamer, loner
- ♥ Watchwords: "I love"
- ♥ Manifestations of the spirit world: Dreams, visions, scents, voices or actions of the deceased

GENERAL

The Page or Princess of Cups is the magical child, the one with the rich and robust fantasy life. She is a dreamer, and she believes in Santa Claus, the Tooth Fairy and the Easter Bunny long after the age at which most children stop believing in such things. The Page of Cups reads Harry Potter, not so much because it is fun and entertaining, but because she believes the things he does are possible. Somewhere there are other kids doing those amazing magical feats, and she dreams that she can become one of that elite group. She has a heart and soul full of wishes and dreams and magical things.

The Page of Cups is usually a very feminine girl or a sensitive boy. Many times the first child, she is attuned to the rationale of adult thinking from a very early age. She can communicate with and win over any adult to her way of thinking just by being sweet, wise and endearing. Because of the enormous amount and level of wisdom exhibited by the Page of Cups at an early age, she is often thought of as an old soul, one with the accumulated wisdom of many lifetimes. When dealing with "reality", she listens intently, thinks carefully and then proceeds cautiously. But the moment reality lets up, she is out riding her unicorn through the magic forest or having tea with the elves.

The Page of Cups is highly creative. She is one of those children who writes elaborate scripts, gathers up her friends to be the cast and performs her production for the neighborhood (she will be the star of course). Cajoling her playmates into going along with one of her ideas is a daily occurrence. Like a little prince or princess, she reigns over them with a velvet touch. But even if they all get into trouble afterward, no one gets angry with her because she would be incredibly wounded and spend days and weeks attempting to make amends.

When other people are sad, the Page of Cups feels their sadness and is filled with empathy for them. She has always been taught to be kind to others and will help in any way she can. She will invite friends for dinner, especially if she knows that they don't have regular meal times at their homes. She will give her coat to someone who is cold. As the Page of Cups gets older she is likely to bring home children in need--kids who don't have as much materially, or who are from dysfunctional families, that she thinks may benefit from her own stable home life. And if her parents object, she will remind them that they taught her to always help and be kind to other people.

As she progresses into her teens, the Page of Cups will be quiet and a bit standoffish. She has many friends from her preteen days, but when she starts to grow up, she is less enthusiastic about standing out in a crowd. Later in her teens, she becomes even less outgoing, a loner of sorts, and chooses one or two really good friends to share her life and to cherish. Striking out into the world at an early age, she perplexes her parents, who see her marching to the tune of a different drummer. But she is anxious to be independent, and the whole world is waiting. She asks for little, and unlike many of her peers, she is content to be introspective, helpful and low key.

She must be held safe by angels, because the Page of Cups usually lives a childhood free of accidents. While other kids are being carted off to the emergency room, she safely traverses her youth. She has relatively few health issues, and does not suffer the usual occurrences of colds and flu. When a student gets an award for not missing a day of school all year, it is likely a Page of Cups.

The Page loves old people. She relishes time with her grandparents, and would rather be with them than with her own parents. This may be due to the fact that her innate wisdom communicates with the wisdom of the aged. She will spend hours with her grandparents, absorbing their stories and experiences. She wants to learn whatever lessons they have to teach her, be it life experience, how to play canasta, how to make a quilt or build a birdhouse. When her grandparents leave her life, she misses them terribly but holds in her heart fond memories of the times she spent with them and the things she learned under their tutelage.

The Page of Cups is not the outdoors type. She is more of a homebody, quite content to spend her days and nights surrounded by her books and her writing. The Page is most happy in the company of her own thoughts and prefers to spend time in her fantasy world rather than facing the reality of homework and cleaning her room.

It is quite likely that the Page of Cups will grow up to be a social worker, a psychologist or a writer. If she chooses social work, it will likely be some sort of geriatric counseling. If she writes, her focus may be social causes and social injustice. She will do her best to make a difference.

THE BASICS:

♦ Sign: Bubbling Brook
♦ Flower: Snapdragon
♦ Gemstone: Blue Topaz
♦ Characteristics: Curious, intellectual, intense
♦ Watchwords: "It makes more sense to do it this way."
♦ Manifestations of the spirit world: Sounds and hearing

GENERAL

The most intellectual and curious child in the Tarot, the Page or Princess of Pentacles was born already grown up. He is bright, highly articulate and intense. He is focused on discovery. The Page wants to know everything there is to know about the world in which he lives. He not only plays with Legos(tm), he creates actual working machines with them, and then he cleans up his mess. The Page is mathematically and mechanically inclined, finding fascination in technology, in electronics, in numbers, and in how things work. He is the child who is capably operating a computer before kindergarten, and who shows Mom how to fix things when she is having computer difficulties. He can't understand why she has a hard time with computers when, for him, it is as natural as breathing.

Along with his intelligence, the Page of Pentacles is often sensitive and high strung. Because of his eager-to-please demeanor and over-achiever personality, when things don't go as planned, his feelings may be hurt. His sensitive nature makes him prone to stress-related illnesses. He is the one who complains of stomach aches before school, and the one who has a veritable rap sheet in the school nurse's office, because every little bump, bruise or scratch is a very big deal. As he matures, his main complaint is tension headaches. A worrier, he is very much in need of a peaceful home life. He likes his own space and spends a lot of time in his room voluntarily, reading, working, discovering new things about the world through books and computer research. He is very attached to his mother and father and has difficulty moving away from home, even when he is beyond his teens.

Usually the Page of Pentacles is born to older or very intelligent parents; the type of parents who played classical music and read poetry to him while he was still in the womb. He is encouraged to be creative, and his parents provide every possible opportunity for his artistic and intellectual advancement. He is sent to a variety of learning camps in the summer, and he is expected to take music lessons. If he wants to learn to play guitar, that is okay with his parents, as long as he learns to play the saxophone or violin as well. Such opportunities are taken in stride because they are nothing more than normal daily occurrences for the Page.

The Page of Pentacles never flaunts his accomplishments, even though he tends to have quite a few more of them than other children do in his age group. But if he is skilled in a task, he will volunteer to perform that task in public. Adults are often surprised when he actually agrees to play his saxophone for the old folks at the nursing home and, rather than sounding like a child playing at something, he sounds like Jr. Walker.

Eventually, like all Pages of Pentacles, he will go to college. He needs to attend school because it fits the image he has of himself and the image he perceives that others have of him. He knows that success is important and, in his almost adult fashion, he will set lofty goals, and he will achieve them. In spite of the incredible pressure to succeed, self-inflicted or otherwise, he is surprisingly well adjusted and doesn't have those quirky emotional problems other kids have.

The Page has many friends, and his friends are almost always as bright as he is. The Page of Pentacles rarely succumbs to peer-pressure. He is much too independent of a thinker to be talked into doing things he knows lead down a path he has no intention of following. He tends not to involve himself in the teenage dating scene simply for the sake of saying he has a girlfriend. When he does date someone, he only picks the cheerleader or homecoming queen if she is highly intelligent and capable of communicating with him on his level. It is not unusual for him to date the smartest girl in the class.

Always encouraged by his parents to participate in a variety of activities (they want him to be well rounded), the Page of Pentacles often excels at singular sports at a very early age. He is most likely a swimmer, tennis player or golfer. When he joins teams sports, he seems to pick the less popular ones such as soccer, lacrosse or volleyball. He is not the true jock-type teenager, but he performs quite well in sports that he enjoys.

The Page is also likely to be the class president, a member of the school concert and marching bands, and the driving force behind the computer club. He is fascinated by technology, and he would be truly upset if he had to go any length of time without his computer. For the Page, it is not a matter of addiction; it is simply his most important tool, because he relies on it for the wealth of information it can and does provide.

The Page of Pentacles is neat and orderly. He is at ease talking to anyone, be it youth or adult. His grace and agility tell the world he is comfortable with himself, confident in his ability, and approachable.

PAGE of SWORDS.

THE BASICS:

- ♠ Sign: Lion Cub
- ♠ Flower: Cornflower
- ♠ Gemstone: Jade
- ♠ Characteristics: Tenacious, intuitive, survivor
- ♠ Watchwords: "I don't really understand the rules."
- ♠ Manifestations of the spirit world: Electrical in nature, lights flickering

GENERAL

The Page or Princess of Swords starts life as a special and challenging child. Who would guess he could grow up to make a notable impact on the world? He normally has a rough beginning, many times reincarnated into a chaotic situation. He is frequently born into an extremely dysfunctional family. Burdened with a broken home, or no real home at all, he seems to wander from place to place, searching for love and acceptance. He learns very early in life that he must fend for himself because no one is going to take care of him.

The Page of Swords is an extremely intuitive child. He instinctively knows who likes him and who does not, but he puts on a brave face, even when rejected. The Page tries to cover his hurt by pretending that somewhere in the world, there is someone who thinks he is special and important and will love him unconditionally. He goes out of his way to be accepted, and is always the one to volunteer to do the things no other child likes, or wants, to do. When the other kids make fun of him because of his clothes, lack of pocket money or for living in a run-down home, he lets it all roll off of his back, because he believes that someday things will magically change. He has never had an elaborate birthday party thrown by loving parents, but is thrilled if he is invited to one. The Page has no hefty allowance and doesn't shop for clothes at the mall. More likely he starts working at about age 12 to earn enough money to buy decent clothes for school. The Page of Swords is not overly bright and often struggles through his schoolwork with no real hope that anyone at home can explain it to him. Undoubtedly, if he had a decent, supportive family environment, things would be a bit different, and he might succeed in his studies. It is, unfortunately, most often not the case.

At times he does things that anger other children, such as revealing their secrets or exaggerating stories. It is never done with malicious intent but only as a bid for attention. In fact, with no decent authority figures to guide him or to explain right from wrong, he may not realize that he is alienating his peers, or why he is alienating them. The Page of Swords lives an amazingly confused childhood.

As he matures, the Page of Swords suddenly changes from an ugly duckling into a beautiful swan. It is as though the laws of universal equality reach out and give him good looks to make up for his lack of great intelligence or a loving family. As he reaches his teens, things become somewhat easier when he realizes that good looks can work in his favor. Even then, he is sometimes so hungry for love and acceptance that he uses his physical attractiveness to garner the attention of the opposite sex. As a result, the Page of Swords often makes bad relationship choices and becomes even more deeply entrenched in sticky problems.

But all is not lost; there is a light at the end of the tunnel. The adult that emerges from this troubled and rather sad childhood is someone very special. He has learned incredible life lessons from his youth, and he makes the transition into maturity with ease and confidence. Personal experience teaches him what is really important in life. It also makes him a compassionate adult. Although there is a chance that he might stray onto the wrong life path, surprisingly, the odds are no greater for him than for a child from a warm and loving family environment.

The Page of Swords is a tenacious survivor, adapting to all circumstances. He weathers a childhood of hardship and becomes an adult who will do his best to bring peace and harmony into the world. He strives to help others in their careers and in their daily lives. Often he is the one that performs remarkable deeds and rescues that turn him into an everyday hero. The mature Page leaves a positive impression on everyone he meets, and is regularly surprised to find out that he unknowingly inspired someone to do better, be a better person or achieve more. If there is a person that could be mistaken for an angel, the mature Page of Swords is the one. Quiet, unassuming, never pompous, he makes a lasting impression and has a positive effect on every life he touches.

PAGE of WANDS.

THE BASICS:

♣ Sign: Baby Bunny
♣ Flower: Daffodil
♣ Gemstone: Pearl
♣ Characteristics: Compassionate, wise, peace-loving
♣ Watchwords: "I can do it myself."
♣ Manifestations of the spirit world: Scents and odors announcing the presence of spirits

GENERAL

The Page or Princess of Wands is the sturdy little daffodil on the edge of the forest, growing up sunny and bright among the larger plants and animals. Quiet and intelligent, she is one who is always observing and learning. Not the least bit afraid to be alone, she enjoys her quiet time, living and reveling in the magic of her own mind.

The Page can always find something to do by herself, often seeking opportunities to be alone, yet, when the mood strikes her, she can be incredibly social. She has an upbeat and energetic personality, which makes it easy to draw other children into her games and fantasies. Brimming over with energy, she excels at sports and other physical activities. The Page of Wands dances, roller blades, rides a bike or plays ball all day long with abandon, and her honest enjoyment of these activities allows her to surpass others without any hint of pretentiousness.

She learns to keep her own counsel at a very early age. Often the Page is the child of divorced or busy parents, and having fun while being alone is her homemade substitution for attention. Her boundless energy and endless imagination ensure that entertaining herself is an easy task.

While attending school, the Page always achieves good grades and social acceptance. The other children are attracted to her sharp mind and charming personality. She won't hesitate to join in a variety of school and extracurricular activities. The Page of Wands likes to be in a leadership role, but she will always graciously concede the role if she knows it is important to someone else. She loves her friends and will do anything for them.

Highly compassionate, the Page of Wands will bring home every stray animal she finds. She loves all types of creatures, and has the innate ability to communicate that love to them. They respond to her positively and they are very loyal to her. The Page has endless patience with her critters, and they allow her to do the most extraordinary things to them. She is the child who can dress up her cats and get them to sit in little chairs so she can have tea party guests! Her dogs will allow her to ride them like ponies or will let themselves be harnessed to pull a sled or drag her down the sidewalk on her roller blades. They are not her pets, they are her friends, and she shares everything with them.

Emotionally, she is very sound; more so than most children. There is nothing shy about her. The Page is very straightforward and will always tell you how she feels about things. If you hurt her feelings, she will not hesitate in bringing it to your attention.

The Page of Wands is very intelligent and mature in her thinking and is often drawn to older people. As she matures, she brings home stray people rather than stray animals. The communication skills she honed on her pets give her an upper hand in relating to adults. Self reliant, she prefers to figure things out on her own, rather than asking for help. Adults are comfortable with her intellect and talents, and they like her because she is not the type of child to pester or make a fuss.

The Page of Wands is adventurous, and she loves to see and try new things. She has no problem spending the night away from home. To her it is not separation from Mom or Dad, it's an exciting trip to a new place. Although diverse, flexible and generally unbiased, she has a strong love and loyalty for family. If you dare to say anything negative about someone she loves, be prepared to hear about your indiscretion in no uncertain terms. The Page is a most loyal little friend, and she will fight for what she thinks is right.

She seems wise beyond her years, and she is an easy child to raise. But sometimes the roles are reversed, and she literally becomes a parent to her parents. She is a fine example of the type of extraordinary wisdom often described by the quote "Out of the mouths of babes". Regardless of her position in the family, she can be counted on to be reasonable, and she sees situations clearly. The Page of Wands, like all Wand people, is a nurturing and compassionate soul. It would be almost impossible not to like this refreshing little creature.

Section 2:

THE MINOR ARCANA

INTRODUCTION TO THE MINOR ARCANA

The Minor Arcana are crucial to every reading. The Minors are rich with meaning, and they detail your soul's journey in its present-day incarnation.

The Cups represent all aspects of your personal relationships, such as love, friendships and business contacts.

The Pentacles are all about the your finances, what you have in the bank or in your possession, what could be coming to you, and, unfortunately, what wealth and material worth could be leaving your hands. They also are a good barometer of how you use wealth in your present life.

The Swords tell the tale of empowerment and about your health and spiritual well being. Because they are a bit more complex, you will note that the descriptions are separated into General, Health and Spiritual.

The Wands portray day-to-day activities, such as your job, travel, home life and extracurricular activities. Job issues are very common when the Wands appear in a reading.

Each of the 40 cards in the Minor Arcana has a Quick List on the first page, so it isn't necessary to read through the entire description section every time you need a little refresher. You will find, once you really know these cards, they will speak volumes to you.

THE SUIT OF CUPS

ACE OF CUPS

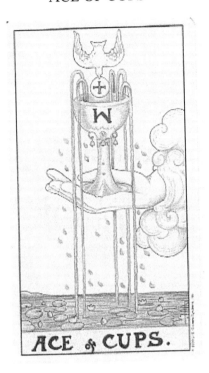

Keyword: Love

Quick List:

Upright
- ♥ Soul mate
- ♥ Unconditional love
- ♥ Heroism
- ♥ Love affair
- ♥ Proposal
- ♥ Extraordinary kindness

Reversed
- ♥ Sad relationship
- ♥ No longer in love
- ♥ Neglected
- ♥ Waning of self worth
- ♥ Love ends

In-Depth:

Upright: The Ace of Cups is the indicator of great love. If you have not yet found your soul mate, you will, and soon. There is a feeling of overwhelming love for those close to you, as in the unconditional love between family members. A wonderful friendship will grow into an even more wonderful love. Marriage proposals are not unusual when the Ace is found in your reading. But the Ace also portends love affairs. Your love relationships are approved by others. It is a time of emotional uplifting and spiritual growth, a time when extraordinary kindness is displayed and heroism is frequent.

Reversed: Love in all its forms is ending when the Ace is reversed. You are no longer in love with the person who loves you, or you are still in love with a person who no longer loves you. Sometimes you feel as though the relationship is hanging by a thread and divorce is a viable choice. It is a sad time, because it heralds the end of what was once a stable, long-term relationship. You feel you have been betrayed by those you love, or perhaps just neglected by a loved one. The uncertainty might cause you to lose faith in yourself or in your beliefs. There is reason for mistrust. If you are entering a new relationship, all may not be what it seems. Be cautious.

TWO OF CUPS

Keyword: Friendship

Quick List:

Upright
♥ Affectionate friendship
♥ Peaceful conclusion
♥ Growing bonds
♥ Same sex liaison
♥ Alternative lifestyles

Reversed
♥ Unstable friend
♥ Disloyalty
♥ Duplicity
♥ Struggle over personal
   decisions
♥ Using one another

In-Depth:

Upright: The Two of Cups inspires a variety of interpretations. An affectionate friendship is indicated in many readings. It also indicates peaceful conclusions to important projects and the growing and strengthening of bonds between two people, often during difficult situations. It bespeaks the powerful bonds forged during a time of severe adversity, such as those formed during a crisis, rescue or hostage situation. It also represents the ideal of being able to count on one's friends. But it also signifies alternative lifestyles and same sex relationships, overcoming social pressures concerning one's sexuality and coming to terms with same sex relationships peacefully; for example, getting past any sort of discrimination or maligning by unenlightened persons.

Reversed: Friendships are questionable when the Two is reversed. All is not as it appears. A friend is unstable, not trustworthy, perhaps even disloyal or duplicitous. If you tell your deepest fears and secrets to this friend you will find your trust betrayed. In a same sex relationship, this card signals possible hurdles to overcome in coming to terms with sexuality. You have difficulty deciding what path to take in that regard. Should you proceed with that sex change operation? Even in heterosexual relationships, this card indicates that important personal decisions are a struggle, such as whether or not to start a family. It is best to put such decisions on the shelf until all other pertinent factors become apparent. It also suggests disregard of a friendship, or using the friendship for personal gain or other ill intentions. In some situations, the Two implies that although you are blind to it yourself, others view your current relationship poorly, and often they counsel you that the match is ill advised.

THREE OF CUPS

Keyword: Celebration

Quick List:

Upright
♥ Joy
♥ End of anger
♥ Good causes
♥ Fund raising
♥ Reunion

Reversed
♥ Too much of a good thing
♥ Friendless
♥ No cause for celebration
♥ Estrangement
♥ Cancellations

In-Depth:

Upright: There is cause for celebration when the Three of Cups appears in the reading. Joy abounds, weddings, parties and reunions are common during this time. It is opportune to hold fund-raising events now, or to participate in any other type of gathering for a good cause. There will be a good outcome to such events. There is great anticipation of happiness. It also indicates the end of cycles of anger. It is time to end the state of estrangement from friends and relatives. If you haven't spoken to a parent or sibling in years, do it now. In the case of adopted children, the Three indicates a possible reunion with one or both birth parents or siblings.

Reversed: Cancellations of planned celebrations are indicated. There is no feeling of joy around you. You are feeling like an outsider, never a member of the clique or the popular crowd. You feel lost and friendless, out of touch with anything of importance or worth. There is estrangement from immediate family members, perhaps for many years, and there is seemingly no hope for a change in that situation. As an adoptive child, you will be unable to find your biological family for the time being. Mild depression and yearning for companionship become a normal state of being when the Three is reversed.

FOUR OF CUPS

Keyword: Dissatisfaction

Quick List:

Upright
- ♥ Boredom
- ♥ Anxiety
- ♥ Too many choices
- ♥ Dissatisfaction
- ♥ Unmotivated
- ♥ Angst

Reversed
- ♥ No tenacity
- ♥ Insecurity
- ♥ Taking risks
- ♥ Excitement coming
- ♥ Unexpected

In-Depth:

Upright: If the Four of Cups appears in the reading, you are likely suffering from both boredom and anxiety. There are many choices available to you right now, but you have no clue which ones would be best. You don't see the possibilities right in front of you. There is a general feeling of angst and fleeting sensations of nonspecific remorse. You seem dissatisfied and discontented with just about everything in your life. It is very hard to tell where you fit right now.

Reversed: The Four reversed will find you making decisions even though you don't know if they are right. You're emerging from a contemplative period and feeling insecure, but you're taking risks in spite of that insecurity. New goals and ambitions are forming in your deepest self. Tenacity is not in your vocabulary; you are no longer holding on to preconceived notions about your life. As a result, exciting things are coming your way, because taking risks and being open to change creates an atmosphere that invites new, different and exciting things into your life.

FIVE OF CUPS

Keyword: Regret

Quick List:

Upright
- ♥ Overly negative
- ♥ Lonely
- ♥ Miserable
- ♥ Sour attitude
- ♥ Poor me
- ♥ Depressed

Reversed
- ♥ Counting blessings
- ♥ Finding the silver lining
- ♥ No anxiety
- ♥ Not lonely
- ♥ Surprised with good fortune

In-Depth:

Upright: The Five of Cups is misery and regret. And you're so sucked down in it that you're unable to do anything positive or reason your way out of the depths. Even when positive things are happening around you, your abject negativity hides the good from your sight. Misery loves company, but you are so completely overwhelmed by it that you feel nothing but loneliness. Additionally, the Five also portends inconsolable grief.

Reversed: Count your blessings! With the Five reversed you will find the silver lining in every cloud. Depression and misery diminish, as everything around you becomes more positive. Loneliness disappears as your improving attitude draws emotionally upbeat people into your circle. If you are thinking the worst, rest easy, the worst is not likely to happen at this time.

SIX OF CUPS

Keyword: Childhood

Quick List:

Upright
♥ Childhood memories
♥ Ancestry
♥ Genealogy
♥ Reunions with old friends
♥ Old friend is new love

Reversed
♥ Painful childhood
♥ Unresolved issues
♥ Escaping past
♥ Child abuse
♥ Incest
♥ No reunions

The Suit of Cups

In-Depth:

Upright: The happy, warm, fuzzy feelings of childhood are prominent when the Six of Cups is found in the reading. Memories of times long past are brought forth, mulled over, discussed and cherished. You find yourself pulling out the old scrapbooks, yearbooks and other memorabilia. It is a good time to study your ancestry, take up genealogy and search for your roots. You find yourself seeing through the eyes of your inner child, and otherwise insignificant events stir up memories. There is opportunity to reacquaint with old friends. Don't be surprised if an old friendship grows into an unexpected love relationship. The Six indicates that a new love is someone from the past.

Reversed: You are not pleased at the family reunion invitation. The Six reversed often indicates an unhappy childhood with many negative memories, and in some cases, may signify child abuse in the past. Your life is rife with unresolved issues from childhood, and you are clinging to grudges over old hurts. It also suggests that you desire escaping your past. You tend to keep a low profile and keep your personal information as private as possible. Taking on a new identity to escape the past, as in changing your name or entering the witness protection program, is also a possibility.

SEVEN OF CUPS

Keyword: Illusions

Quick List:

Upright
- ♥ Gifts
- ♥ Compliments
- ♥ Appreciation
- ♥ Daydreaming
- ♥ Wishing
- ♥ Psychic ability

Reversed
- ♥ Lack of creativity
- ♥ Fragmented thinking
- ♥ Not believing in self
- ♥ Loss of important things
- ♥ Deception

In-Depth:

Upright: The Seven of Cups is a fun card to have in your reading. It is the gift card. For no apparent reason, this is the cycle in life when people just seem to give you things. Compliments are common, as are thanks, gestures of appreciation and tokens of affection. Gifts of jewelry are the order of the day. You are surrounded by the spirits of people who love you. It is a time of creative daydreaming, wishing and hoping, believing in magic. You visualize magical or unrealistic things happening to you. Psychic abilities come to the forefront of your daily living. Astral projection, precognition and premonition become commonplace.

Reversed: You have been kicked a few times and didn't like it much. Now you are feeling down and no longer believe that you can accomplish your goals or achieve your dreams. All seems lost. Frustration plagues you, as attempts to think your way out of the situation are less than successful. Fragmented thinking is party to the problem. But there could be other unseen things at work. Deception may add to the situation and, not knowing other forces are at odds with your plan, you find yourself fighting the unknown and invisible. The Seven reversed also indicates drug use and substance abuse.

EIGHT OF CUPS

Keyword: Restless Journey

Quick List:

Upright
- ♥ Interference by another person
- ♥ Wandering
- ♥ Wrong path
- ♥ Abandoning all
- ♥ Seeking birth parents

Reversed
- ♥ Relationships not threatened
- ♥ Significant other is faithful
- ♥ Regretting leaving
- ♥ Not able to leave
- ♥ Together for the kids

In-Depth:

Upright: Life is a journey, and the Eight of Cups is a wandering card. This is not the card of vacation travels. You are searching for fulfillment and trying to balance your relationships to keep things running on an even keel. But something is missing. There is interference in your relationships by a third party. Straying from the original path, you are uncertain about whether to stay in the situation or leave. After lingering too long in a difficult situation, you are tempted to abandon it all and start fresh. If adopted, you embark on the journey to find your birth parents.

Reversed: Your relationship is not in danger from another person (he isn't cheating on you). That does not mean the situation isn't strained. You are staying in the relationship for other reasons, such as stability for the children or financial concerns. Perhaps you are afraid to take the leap of faith required to go it alone, or fear that you are incapable of earning enough money to survive. If the relationship is abusive, you might be brainwashed into thinking you can't live without him. It's time to let go of the bad situation when the Eight is reversed.

NINE OF CUPS

Keyword: Wish Card

In-Depth:

Upright: Make a wish! The Nine of Cups is the card of wishes. There is happiness in your life as goals are achieved and dreams become reality. Everything is working out just the way you planned. You have abundance in all areas: good health, emotional balance, spiritual harmony and physical wellness. If you have a wish, the Nine answers the question positively. Will I stay the course? Will I finish school? Will I lose weight? Will I quit smoking? Will I find love? Upright, the Nine says "yes" your wish will be fulfilled.

Reversed: When the Nine is reversed, it becomes a "don't bother making any wishes" card. It is just not happening for you right now. Forestall making plans because they will not come to fruition. The failure of diets, plans and physical goals has you drowning your sorrows. You are overindulging, overeating and exhibiting greed and disregard (for yourself and for others). You find there really can be too much of a good thing. Use common sense and stop punishing yourself with your behaviors.

TEN OF CUPS

Keyword: Joy

Quick List:

Upright
♥ Blessed marriage
♥ Joy in home
♥ Finding soul mate
♥ Blessings
♥ Good relationships

Reversed
♥ Rocky relationship
♥ Separation
♥ Possible divorce
♥ Child leaves nest

In-Depth:

Upright: There is joy in your home. The Ten of Cups indicates blessed marriages, blissful relationships and happy households. If you are not yet married, a promise of marriage could be forthcoming. You have found or will find your soul mate. Parents and children are living in harmony. Everyone is healthy, happy and safe. What more could you ask for?

Reversed: Things are heading down the rocky path in your relationship when the Ten is reversed. There is a possible separation or divorce in the offing if considerable attention is not paid to the relationship in question. The happiness in your home is disrupted by separations. Your son joins the service and heads overseas turning you into a nervous wreck. Your daughter is caught shoplifting and goes to jail or marries some lowdown criminal type and leaves home. Or one of your parents dies. These types of situations cause great distress and unhappiness, so grit your teeth and hang in there a while; things will settle down.

THE SUIT OF PENTACLES

ACE OF PENTACLES

Keyword: Wealth

Quick List:

Upright
♦ Wealth
♦ Financial success
♦ Ability to create wealth
♦ Prosperity
♦ Visionary acquisitions
♦ Adept in financial

Reversed
♦ Loss of wealth
♦ Stock market losses
♦ Poor financial management
♦ Ill-gotten gains
♦ Expected windfall will not
  come about

In-Depth:

Upright: Regardless of whether you prefer using an archaic or current interpretation, the Ace of Pentacles simply means money. When this card appears in the upright position, it indicates that you have, or will have, money or material wealth, or that you possess the ability to draw money and material wealth to yourself. This could indicate impending successful projects and financial health. It is a good time for investments. You have the ability to create prosperity, individually and in your career. It could also indicate that you will have the means necessary for buying the things you need or desire. You have a healthy love of abundance; you are goal-oriented in your quest for wealth. You also exhibit visionary thinking, as in creating new ways to acquire possessions. Good money management is indicated.

Reversed: The Ace reversed is the loss of money. Money is constantly slipping through your fingers. You have no idea where it all went. There is generally poor money management afoot. Sometimes the money goes out as fast, if not faster, than it comes in. Watch your stocks, as this card could indicate stock market losses and the bottoming out of investments. Don't count on that money that you think is coming in, because it is likely you will be disappointed and financially devastated. On the other hand, the Ace reversed can suggest the evil side of money. Be wary of ill-gotten gains or money that was acquired illegally or immorally. Watch out for insider trading. It could also mean that you are using money for bad ends, such as laundering money or financing criminal activity.

TWO OF PENTACLES

Keyword: Imbalance

Quick List:

Upright
♦ Imbalance
♦ Juggling
♦ Coveting
♦ Insufficient income
♦ Foolish spending

Reversed
♦ Resolution
♦ Money smarts
♦ Money education
♦ Successful budgeting
♦ Wisdom in spending

In-Depth:

Upright: The Two of Pentacles indicates financial imbalance. You don't have enough coming in to cover your expenses, or you are headed in that direction. Considerable time is spent juggling money, often robbing Peter to pay Paul, or calling the bank daily to check your balance because you're living on the float. Oftentimes you seem unable to make wise purchases and find for sale later things for which you paid a premium. You find that you are very envious of what others have that you cannot afford. When you do find the needed item on sale, you either can't afford to buy it, or you increase your debt load by charging it, which only causes...more imbalance.

Reversed: For this card, a reversed position is a hopeful sign. There is or will be a resolution of those troubling money issues. You learn to make wise money decisions and to balance your income with your expenditures. Don't be surprised if you find yourself in a class on personal financial management or frequently glued to some late night TV show touting financial management experts. You will use any newly gained knowledge to pay off your loans and lower your credit card debts. Financial stability is in the offing.

THREE OF PENTACLES

Keyword: Education

Quick List:

Upright
♦ Teacher
♦ Student
♦ New ideas
♦ Finance classes
♦ College

Reversed
♦ No follow through
♦ Delay in schooling
♦ Unprepared
♦ Lacking skills
♦ Stagnation

In-Depth:

Upright: Ready to teach or learn? When the Three of Pentacles appears, there is a learning experience on the way, particularly in regards to financial matters. Whether you are the teacher or the student, the lessons will result in financial benefit. Often this card indicates a college education or other advanced learning. The path from the education to the money is indirect. For example, you go to college and earn a degree. The degree enables you to get a better job. The job stimulates your creativity and the ideas stemming from that creativity result in a financial windfall. Some people have a degree and never use it to their advantage. This card indicates that the potential is there to make the education pay off. Don't be afraid to ask the advice of experts. You will gain valuable knowledge in the process.

Reversed: You are fully capable of success, but you lack the drive to gain the skills required to achieve that success. Must do tasks are done half-heartedly and without enthusiasm. You tend to want things handed to you rather than earning them. Chances are you will delay your education (taking off a semester to make money working) and then procrastinate returning to school until it seems too late. Or you might be in college, but feel no need to work hard, turn in assignments on time or get anything more than a passing grade. In your employment, you often attempt to accomplish tasks without having sufficient preparation to succeed. This generally results in failure, blotting your work record and your hopes for advancement and raises. You know your capabilities are limitless; you can achieve what you set out to do. Although you want the adulation and monetary reward you feel you deserve, you fail to follow through and habitually neglect doing what's necessary to accomplish the goal.

FOUR OF PENTACLES

Keyword: Frugality

Quick List:

Upright	Reversed
♦ Miserly	♦ Careless
♦ Hoarding	♦ Irresponsible
♦ Pack rat	♦ Late payments
♦ Uncharitable	♦ Frivolous spending
♦ Insecurity	♦ Political graft

In-Depth:

Upright: It could be a long-term condition or one just newly developed, but the Four of Pentacles in a reading portends greed and insecurity. Frugality is normally an asset, but you could be taking it to extremes. Your need to hold onto everything you've ever owned, including your first communion money, is driving your spouse, family, significant other or roommate completely crazy. You're giving new meaning to the term pack rat. Unfortunately you also exhibit Scrooge-like behavior, holding on to every penny while callously ignoring the plight of those less fortunate. If you are a successful career woman, you could be suffering from "bag-lady syndrome", the fear of losing everything you've managed to earn or save. Life becomes a scrimp-and-save scenario. This can cause you to act in ways you would normally never dream of acting, such as: drying out and reusing teabags or paper towels; limiting the number of squares of toilet paper you can use at a sitting; or meticulously measuring the food you are serving to make sure everyone gets no more than one exact portion.

Reversed: Just as frugality can be taken to extremes (upright card), letting go of money and the associated worries swings too far in the opposite direction. You become careless with money, especially in dealing with financial obligations. Responsibility takes a holiday as you go out and buy that huge plasma screen TV or gas-guzzling SUV, conveniently ignoring important debts, like your mortgage payments. You consistently procrastinate paying bills, allowing added late fees and interest to increase your debts. Bribery and political graft are also indicated.

FIVE OF PENTACLES

Keyword: Old Age

Quick List:

Upright
♦ Charity
♦ Loss of money
♦ Loss of job
♦ Destitution
♦ Homelessness

Reversed
♦ Old age duo
♦ Enduring relationships
♦ Struggling through
♦ Persisting
♦ Surviving

In-Depth:

Upright: A generally negative card, the Five of Pentacles portends the loss of money. You could get bilked out of your life savings, lose your job or other sources of income, or worse yet, you might lose your ability to earn a living. This could be a long-term situation, so be prepared for such an eventuality. Heavy financial burdens, bankruptcy, homelessness and the state of total destitution are possible. Swallow your pride; you need to rely on the charity of others to get by.

Reversed: The prominent meaning of the Five reversed is old age together. Your relationship will be enduring, even through the hard times and all the financial uncertainties. Together you continue to go forward in spite of adversity. Overall, the card indicates any relationship of great length. This refers not only to intimate partnerships, but to long-term friendships as well as lengthy business partnerships or client relationships.

SIX OF PENTACLES

Keyword: Balance

Quick List:

Upright
♦ Generosity
♦ Spreading the wealth
♦ Philanthropy
♦ Laws of abundance
♦ Financial balance
♦ Sharing

Reversed
♦ Stinginess
♦ Con man
♦ Bilking the unaware
♦ Taking from the needy

In-Depth:

Upright: The Six of Pentacles is a card most everyone would love to have pop up in a reading. It represents balanced money. You have firm control over the income and outflow. Your attitudes toward wealth are healthy, with no evidence of avarice or greed. The Laws of Abundance are foremost in your thoughts, and you know that in order to keep balance you need to give back. With adequate resources at your disposal, you champion causes and help others. Others consider you to be a philanthropist or you are well on your way to becoming one. This card indicates the ability and desire to use wealth for good, such as setting up foundations and charitable institutions with no thought of personal gain. You know how to share the wealth and proceed to do so regularly.

Reversed: Cheap, cheap, cheap: The Six in this position can indicate that you are extremely unwilling to share what you have or give to others even if you can see their plight. It also indicates that though you have been entrusted with the responsibility of taking care of other people's money, you are irresponsible with it, abusing that trust, usually for your own gain. Illegal wrangling of stocks and profiting from insider trading to the detriment of others both apply. Some major corporate-type scandals come to mind, such as the Enron debacle, embezzling pension funds, investment fraud, selling off stocks the day before a company goes bust and generally making sure you get yours even if people who trusted you lose everything.

SEVEN OF PENTACLES

Keyword: Worry

Quick List:

Upright
♦ Worry
♦ Unfounded anxiety
♦ Guarding money
♦ Cultivating wealth
♦ Watching money grow

Reversed
♦ Worry is founded
♦ Carelessness
♦ Not worrying when you
  should

In-Depth:

Upright: It seems like all you ever do is worry about money, finances and bills. With the Seven of Pentacles, you are worrying in the face of plenty. You have enough to cover things but keep worrying anyway. Those fears are unfounded. Time spent anxiously guarding what you have could be spent on more productive pursuits. It is likely that you have money in many areas, stocks, bonds, investments and other funds. But babysitting those investments tends to be overkill. You are worrying about losing what most people don't even have.

Reversed: The Seven reversed indicates that you should be worried about your finances, but you don't seem to have a care in the world. Take some time to check up on your money or you could be in trouble. This card position could also mean that you should stop worrying about how you will pay for something, the money will be there when you need it.

EIGHT OF PENTACLES

Keyword: Trade

Quick List:

Upright
♦ Trades
♦ Vocations
♦ Blue collar
♦ Training
♦ Workforce education
♦ Repetition

Reversed
♦ Lack of training
♦ Misuse of talents
♦ Hacking
♦ Counterfeiting
♦ Burglary

In-Depth:

Upright: The Eight of Pentacles indicates education, but generally vocational training as opposed to college. It would be a good time to prepare for skilled labor jobs, such as plumbing, heat and air conditioning, auto repair or computer technology. Tapping your vocational skills and artistic talent could bring you financial success, but you need to hone those skills and upgrade your knowledge in those areas to make the most of the opportunities that present themselves. Don't be afraid of repetition. It might seem boring, but repetition leads to perfection.

Reversed: Lack of training and education in your vocation is holding you back. You are not using your talents to the level of your capability, and additional education could be the catalyst for advancement. Unfortunately, the Eight reversed can also indicate using your talents to bad ends. Instead of selling your paintings like other starving artists, you're painting forgeries for fast and easy income. Your manual dexterity has you safe cracking and committing cat burglary rather than constructing intricate circuit boards or computer chips. And then, there is the ever-popular computer hacker, using his profound knowledge of computer hardware and software to cause disruption all across the Internet, just for the fun of it. It also indicates the presence of a mischievous repeat offender or petty criminal, the good-natured and charming thief or kleptomaniac.

NINE OF PENTACLES

Keyword: Pleasure

Quick List:

Upright	**Reversed**
♦ Pleasure	♦ Theft
♦ Financially secure	♦ Loss
♦ Independent	♦ Risk taking
♦ Self-reliant	♦ Excessive gambling
♦ Set apart from others	
♦ Lonely	

In-Depth:

Upright: While the Nine of Pentacles is about pleasure from material wealth, it is not about pleasure without pain. It is likely that you are financially secure. You have all that you need and more. People envy your independence, material wealth and seeming to "have it all" in these areas they find lacking in their own lives. But your pleasure is tainted. Though you sit, surrounded by all your belongings, you are alone with your possessions. In this case, pleasure does not equate to happiness. It is a lonely card, generally because it is difficult to know if someone likes you for yourself or for your money; therefore, you tend to remain set apart from others socially and emotionally.

Reversed: The reversed position of the Nine has only negative connotations. It portends loss of material possessions in most of its forms. But it also indicates loss of security, the onset of poor financial standing or devaluation of your retirement funds. The loss can be accidental, as in diving stock values, or deliberate as in theft of your belongings. It is not a good time for investments, especially questionable ones. Keep your money close to the vest and avoid challenging or risking your financial security. It would also be good to avoid Las Vegas, Atlantic City, Windsor, Niagara Falls and the local racetrack or bingo hall as you will end up gambling away funds that are necessary to meet your financial obligations.

TEN OF PENTACLES

Keyword: Inheritance

Quick List:

Upright
♦ Inheriting
♦ Bestowing
♦ Passing skills
♦ Passing heirlooms
♦ Legacy

Reversed
♦ Unusual inheritance
♦ Unexpected windfall
♦ Loss of estate
♦ Family secrets
♦ Black sheep

In-Depth:

Upright: The Ten of Pentacles might be your card of fortune. Whether the inheritor or the bestower, this card indicates giving with "warm" hands. In essence, the gift is both given and received in love. The inheritance can be money, either passed after death or assigned before death by a parent or grandparent. The card also indicates a loving benefactor who will provide you with emergency cash in a pinch. But the inheritance or gift might not be money at all. It could be family heirlooms: Aunt Hilda's brooch and Great Grandma's mahogany rocking chair. It also covers the acquisition of auction items (either in person or on-line). Or it could represent the passing of land, house, real property, stock portfolios or a family business--a legacy handed down through generations. It also indicates the passing of skills from one generation to the next, especially skills that allow one to earn a living, such as baking, jewelry making, diamond cutting, lock-smithing and tailoring, to name just a few. Overall, it means the wealth is coming full cycle as it passes from one hand to another.

Reversed: There are two sides to the Ten of Pentacles reversed. On one hand, it portends the unexpected gain. You could be the recipient of an unusual inheritance. Perhaps you did someone a favor long ago, and suddenly you find that person has remembered you in his will. It also represents the unexpected windfall...the IRS finds a mistake on your tax returns and you get additional money back; you are the one-millionth customer and are awarded some type of money or merchandise. On the other hand, this card can indicate the loss of inheritance. Someone contests a will and your cut is reduced or negated. There could be a secret regarding the family fortune, such as it all came from bootlegging. A trusted party might have used the estate for personal gain or in some other underhanded manner. It can simply indicate the black sheep of the family. Or it could mean the loss of family heirlooms, by accident, subterfuge or necessity (as in selling them to satisfy financial obligations). In some readings, the Ten reversed indicates racial bias. In extreme circumstances, it could mean the loss of pension funds.

THE SUIT OF SWORDS

ACE OF SWORDS

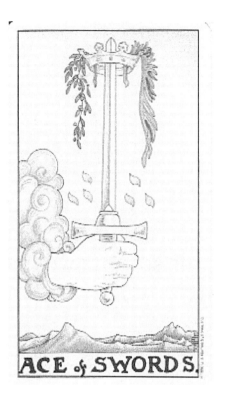

Keyword: Power

Quick List:

Upright
- ♠ Power of self
- ♠ In charge
- ♠ Ready for the challenge
- ♠ Good health
- ♠ Spiritual
- ♠ Leadership

Reversed
- ♠ Loss of power
- ♠ Follower
- ♠ Not in control
- ♠ Illness
- ♠ Lack of faith in self

In-Depth:

Upright - General: Traditionally, the Ace of Swords represented the triumph of physical force and victory in battle. Today swords stand for power, and the Ace upright means you are holding your power in your own hands. Now is the time for taking command of your destiny. You are charging forward with your eyes wide open. There are challenges ahead, but you are ready to do what is necessary to reach the goal. **Health:** The Ace of Swords depicts good physical and mental heath. It also indicates recovery from illness, increase in energy and return of former stamina, giving you power over the physical obstacles you encounter. **Spiritual:** The Ace indicates extraordinary spirituality. You have incredible faith in yourself and in your ability to achieve whatever goals you set for yourself.

Reversed - General: You have given up and allowed others to rule your life. The Ace reversed indicates you have relinquished your personal power and are now at the mercy of those who have taken the power. No longer in control, you are following the dictates of others rather than leading down your own path. **Health:** Generally, the Ace reversed portends serious illness. The position it takes in relation to the other cards in the reading indicates type of surgery or a serious problem with a particular part of the body. The Ace reversed also indicates vanity surgery. This could be anything from eye-lift surgery to body art (tattoos) and piercing. **Spiritual:** When the Ace is reversed, you have no faith in your abilities and rightly so. Assignation of your power to others leaves you incapable of controlling your destiny. Your value system is totally askew, and you lose faith in your ability to succeed.

TWO OF SWORDS

Keyword: Unseen Complications

Quick List:

Upright
- ♠ Choices
- ♠ Hidden influences
- ♠ Secrets
- ♠ Ulterior motives
- ♠ Eye-health problems
- ♠ Refusing to seek help

Reversed
- ♠ Taking off the blinders
- ♠ Learning from mistakes
- ♠ Decision making
- ♠ Minor eye health issues
- ♠ Seeking guidance

In-Depth:

Upright - General: The Two of Swords is the double-edged sword. You have choices to make, and it is possible to choose the wrong one, so you must be prudent and careful. Hidden influences may affect the outcome of your choice. There are secrets and pitfalls around you, and you are blinded regarding the motives of people who are not what they seem. But you are also blind to you own faults. You don't see yourself as others see you. Now is not the time to choose by emotion. Put your feelings aside, find reliable advice and think things through. There is hidden danger in the water at this time; watch for jellyfish, sharks and piranha if you plan a trip to the ocean. **Health:** Problems with the eyes are prominent. It is a good time to get checked for glaucoma, macular degeneration, cataracts and diabetic retinopathy. The Two also indicates throat problems, including carotid arteries and thyroid. **Spiritual:** At this time, you are stubbornly refusing to accept that you need guidance. Wake up and smell the roses, but be sure they really are roses before sticking your nose in the bloom.

Reversed - General: The Two reversed indicates that you are letting go of preconceived notions and taking off those blinders. You have learned from your mistakes and have moved beyond previous disastrous choices. Allowing yourself the freedom to be decisive again relieves a long-carried burden of indecision. **Health:** Eye health is still an issue, but to a much lesser degree. You need new glasses, or you have allergies affecting the eyes. Eyestrain is common, as are tonsillitis, swollen glands and sore throats. **Spiritual:** You recognize the need to seek help. Follow up on that instinct.

THREE OF SWORDS

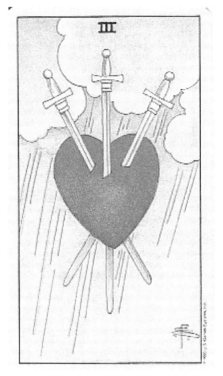

Keyword: Problems of the Heart

Quick List:

Upright
- ♠ Sorrow
- ♠ Grief
- ♠ Heartache
- ♠ Indicators of future heart disease
- ♠ Hanging on to hurts
- ♠ Refusing to move on

Reversed
- ♠ Expected grief will not occur
- ♠ No breakup
- ♠ Good prognosis
- ♠ Need lifestyle changes
- ♠ Accepting loss

In-Depth:

Upright - General: The Three of Swords is the card of sorrow. You are grieving over a loss, be it a loss of loved one, a broken heart or anything otherwise dear to your heart that is no longer viable. This includes job loss and deaths of pets. **Health:** The Three indicates the lead-ins to heart disease. It is time to get checked for high blood pressure, cholesterol, triglycerides and diabetes, all of which can figure prominently in eventual heart problems. **Spiritual:** You are hanging on to past hurts well beyond the normal time of recovery. Grief is extended and intense longer than is healthy. It is time to let go of grief and hurt and find a way to move on with your life.

Reversed - General: The Three reversed indicates that the grief and heartbreak you were dreading will not come to pass. There will be no breakup and no divorce. Stop worrying; it is a waste of your time and energy. **Health:** You are putting yourself on the fast track to future heart disease-related problems. It doesn't have to come to that, you have the power to change your lifestyle before it rules you. Quit smoking, improve your diet, exercise and find ways to lower your stress level to put yourself on a preferable path. Stay away from stinging insects, they might be attracted to you now. **Spiritual:** You have learned acceptance. Letting go of heartache and sorrow, you are getting back to the task of living.

FOUR OF SWORDS

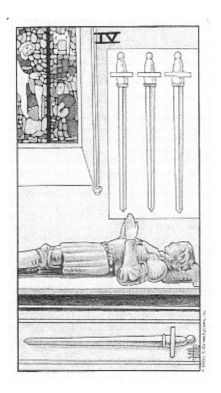

Keyword: Healing Prayer

Quick List:

Upright
- ♠ Prayer
- ♠ Healing sleep
- ♠ Letting go to higher power
- ♠ Sleep on your problems
- ♠ Dreams of direction
- ♠ Creative inspiration

Reversed
- ♠ Spiritual neglect
- ♠ Defying your morality
- ♠ Justifying your actions
- ♠ Sleep problems
- ♠ Unsettling dreams

In-Depth:

Upright - General: The Four of Swords is the prayer card. It indicates that you allow all the negative things in your life to be put to rest through prayer. Coping is best accomplished at present by giving your problems and dangers to a higher power. When you give up that worry, you will feel renewed. The universe will take its course. Trust in the higher power and everything will turn out correctly. **Health:** The peaceful resolution of problems allows you to experience restful and healing sleep. If you are experiencing health problems or stress issues--sleep on them. They will be resolved. **Spiritual:** You acknowledge the existence of a higher power and allow yourself to rely on it for support. Becoming aware of the inner voice that guides you is part of that spiritual awakening. Even in sleep, you receive dreams of direction and creative inspiration for use in your daily life. Heed your dreams.

Reversed - General: When the Four appears reversed, you are neglecting your spiritual side. You are not listening to your inner voice, and you are doing things that defy your own morality, things you know are not right. And you persist in justifying your actions against your better judgement. **Health:** Sleep problems are common, such as snoring, sleep apnea and narcolepsy. If you are tired all the time, a sleep clinic may help solve the problem. **Spiritual:** You are experiencing a lack of faith and have become restless; perhaps even not sleeping well at this time. Precognitive dreaming leaves you feeling unsettled, as do nightmares with messages. Listen to your dreams, they are warning you.

FIVE OF SWORDS

Keyword: Self-satisfaction

Quick List:

Upright	Reversed
♠ Smugness	♠ Thwarted by another's deceit
♠ Win by deceit	♠ No spirit to fight
♠ Ladder climbing	♠ Could have prevented but didn't
♠ Dishonest methods	♠ Minor problems with extremities
♠ Problems with extremities	
♠ Defeated by worry	

In-Depth:

Upright - General: The Five of Swords is the card of the victor and the loser. But regardless of the outcome, the battle was not fought honorably. You got what you wanted and now you are gloating. But you didn't win on your merits, you won by dishonesty and deceit. This could take many forms, such as lying, cheating or spreading rumors about the opposition. These tactics are often found in politics and management, but can be applied to any situation. Perhaps you have become a ladder climber to get ahead, or you have used your sexuality to gain ground (sleeping your way to the top). **Health:** Wrist and shoulder injuries are common, such as torn rotator cuff, bone spurs or carpal tunnel syndrome. Surgery could be indicated. Leg problems are also a possibility, including circulation issues, varicose veins and persistent edema. You have allowed a negative health situation to go on for far too long. It's time to get that check up. **Spiritual:** You are spiritually defeated by earthly concerns and worries, such as work and bills. You need to reevaluate priorities.

Reversed - General: The Five reversed indicates that you have allowed yourself to be thwarted by another's deception. Walk away from the situation; it matters more to them than to you. The energy to fight for what you believe in is lost. What you prized is gone and you did not fight to prevent it from happening. **Health:** Minor health issues are bothering you, such as arthritis, tendonitis, bunions, bursitis and foot, knee, wrist or shoulder pain. **Spiritual:** You are more concerned with material than spiritual and with self-satisfaction than with doing what is right. Again, you need to reevaluate priorities.

SIX OF SWORDS

Keyword: Departure

Quick List:

Upright
- ♠ Sorrowful leaving
- ♠ Separation
- ♠ Divorce
- ♠ Regret leaving the past
- ♠ Stamina
- ♠ New spiritual journey

Reversed
- ♠ Fighting the inevitable
- ♠ Lack of mental preparation
- ♠ Lose faith in children
- ♠ Waning of strength
- ♠ Can't accept need for change

In-Depth:

Upright - General: The Six of Swords represents sorrowful leaving. A child goes off to the service or other destinations for months if not years. Or the family could otherwise be torn apart by separation or divorce. You regretfully leave the past behind, although you know you go forward into a better life. Even in sorrow you have the ability to create a new life for yourself. The Six also represents a journey over water. **Health:** You have enough physical strength for yourself as well as for others. You've moved away from poor health habits by changing diet and exercising more, and your stamina has increased. You are a positive influence on the health habits of others. Don't be surprised to find yourself taking a path to becoming a nutritionist, dietician or personal trainer. **Spiritual:** You are steering yourself, or allowing yourself to be directed, toward a better spiritual path. A new spiritual journey awaits you.

Reversed - General: When the Six is reversed, you are fighting against the inevitable. It is a losing battle and you are wasting your energies. Something is coming, and though you know it, you are not mentally preparing yourself. There are cancellations of journey or travel plans. Discoveries about your children will shake your faith in them and in what you taught them (drugs, alcohol, running with the wrong crowd). Also, be cautious of your children around strangers, abductions are possible. The Six can portend returning home after a separation. **Health:** There is waning of physical strength. You return to bad health habits (smoking, overeating). **Spiritual:** You are unable to accept the need for positive change and have lost faith in former beliefs.

SEVEN OF SWORDS

Keyword: Theft

Quick List:

Upright
♠ Theft
♠ Identity fraud
♠ Plagiarism
♠ Cut and run
♠ Upper body difficulties
♠ Morals askew

Reversed
♠ Risk of loss diminished
♠ The lost is returned
♠ Mended relationships
♠ Health improves
♠ Moral priorities restored

In-Depth:

Upright - General: A complex card, the Seven of Swords is often known as the theft card. Be wary of all your possessions, don't be careless at this time. This applies to not only material things and money, but to your ideas and your identity. Your energy could be stolen by problems and obstacles on work projects causing setbacks. Or you are just at your wit's end holding the project together and should take what you have left and run. Your power is diluted by the actions of others. Loss of integrity is possible. **Health:** The upper body gets the brunt of it when the Seven appears. Be wary of upper respiratory conditions (such as chronic bronchitis, pneumonia, emphysema) that appear or seem to linger. Breast cancer could also be of imminent concern, as well as shoulder, neck or extremity pain that requires surgical correction. **Spiritual:** You are not thinking or acting in a righteous way. Time to reassess and re-evaluate your moral priorities.

Reversed - General: The Seven reversed indicates a lessening of all the previously negative things. The risk of material loss is diminished. Your thoughts and ideas will remain sacred to you. The time is ripe for making changes and decisions. Financial losses will be recouped. Your integrity will no longer be challenged. Broken friendships will mend. Lost or stolen property will be recovered. When the Seven is reversed, all that is lost will be returned to you. **Health:** Physical problems are on the mend. Any complaints that arise are minor in nature, such as minor joint pains, allergies, cold or flu bugs. **Spiritual:** Your thinking returns to its former path. Mental health is optimal and your morals remain intact.

EIGHT OF SWORDS

Keyword: Bondage

Quick List:

Upright
- ♠ Bondage
- ♠ Imprisonment
- ♠ Obsession
- ♠ Gastrointestinal problems
- ♠ Losing the moral path

Reversed
- ♠ Letting go addictions
- ♠ Release from prison
- ♠ Minor stomach woes
- ♠ Finding your moral self
- ♠ Reverting to the
  non-obsessive

In-Depth:

Upright - General: The Eight of Swords represents bondage in all its forms. You are immobile, imprisoned within yourself, as addictions (yours or those of others) rule your life. Obsession and obsessive relationships are often seen with this card. Stalking behavior is possible at this time. You are often blind to the negative aspects of others. Avoid places where you could inadvertently become a hostage. Use caution. A jail term could also be imminent. But you are just as likely to be a prisoner of illness or obesity or any number of other problems. **Health:** Watch for digestive difficulties, stress incontinence, irritable bowel syndrome, colitis and gall stones. Urinary tract infections as well as stomach, liver and pancreas problems are also common, as are eating disorders. The Eight can also portend gastric by-pass surgery. **Spiritual:** You are not paying a bit of attention to what is morally correct. You are so bound by negative addictions that you turn your back on God, family or upbringing. Allowing those negative influences to take precedence leads you down an evil path.

Reversed - General: You let go of addictions and the things that bind you when the Eight is reversed. Release from prison or a hostage situation is possible. **Health:** Minor gastrointestinal problems, such as acid reflux, heartburn, hiatal hernia, indigestion or flu that causes stomach symptoms, are the order of the day. **Spiritual:** You have let go of the negative and are coming back to the self you know is morally correct. Reverting to non-obsessive behavior allows light back into your life, heart and soul.

NINE OF SWORDS

Keyword: Grief

Quick List:

Upright	**Reversed**
♠ Guilt	♠ Anxiety decreases
♠ Worry	♠ Restful sleep resumes
♠ Anxiety	♠ Stress symptoms disappear
♠ Grief	♠ Don't worry about it
♠ Stress-related illnesses	
♠ Anxiety outweighs beliefs	

In-Depth:

Upright - General: The Nine of Swords is the card of guilt and worry. Anxiety and fear are ruining your sleep, leading to depression and lack of concentration. You could experience negative dreams, and you have grave concerns over loved ones. This includes their safety, health or decision making. You have worries over the death or loss of a loved one. Inevitably you take on the problems of the world. Seeing the despairing side of every person down on their luck, you try to fix them and take on the worry that belongs to them alone. **Health:** Tension and stress of unnecessary worries and guilt bring on panic attacks, migraine headaches, neck tension and heart palpitations (not heart disease). Ulcers and all manner of stress-related illness are common. Watch for epilepsy and other neuro-electrical malfunctions. **Spiritual:** You allow anxiety and fear to pervade your mind regardless of your beliefs to the contrary. You are dwelling on the negative. Trust your beliefs and let go of the anxiety.

Reversed - General: There is lessening of anxiety. You release the worry that plagues you and sound sleep returns. **Health:** Generally speaking, when conflict leaves, when worry and anxiety end, most symptoms will disappear. **Spiritual:** You refuse to surrender to feelings of depression. Your entire frame of mind is improved as you let go of anxiety.

TEN OF SWORDS

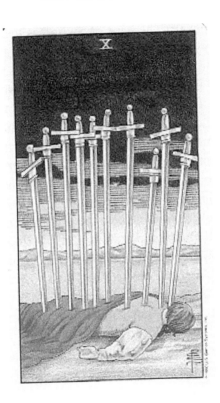

Keyword: Pain

Quick List:

Upright
- ♠ Pain
- ♠ Stabbed in the back
- ♠ Defeated
- ♠ Back pain
- ♠ Arthritis
- ♠ Despairing

Reversed
- ♠ Reputation cleared
- ♠ Recovery
- ♠ Life is improving
- ♠ Minor back issues
- ♠ Positive attitude

In-Depth:

Upright - General: The Ten of Swords is the card of pain. But the pain can be physical or come in other forms. You have had a painful ending of a relationship or job. Or you've been stabbed in the back by someone you trusted. You've been victimized by scandal, libel or slander. Overcome by the negative, you are completely defeated. Major setbacks are likely. Tragic loss is possible. **Health:** Serious back pain, caused by herniated discs, scoliosis, lordosis or spinal malformations are indicated. Any of these could result in back surgery. But the back pain might also be caused by lymphomas, fibromyalgia, lupus, rheumatoid arthritis, even kidney stones or ovarian cysts. If your back hurts, seek medical advice. **Spiritual:** You are disconsolate and have given up. Mental pain has led you to despair and you've accepted failure. There is no light at the end of the tunnel.

Reversed - General: Your reputation is restored. Problems that seemed insurmountable in the past now are easily resolved. There is successful recovery from serious health issues. Life is improving. **Health:** Back issues are still prominent, but are of a much less serious nature, such as sciatica, sprain or strain, pinched nerves or osteoarthritis. **Spiritual:** You do not allow yourself to be defeated by the negatives in life. Keeping a positive demeanor allows you to face difficulties and triumph.

THE SUIT OF WANDS

ACE OF WANDS

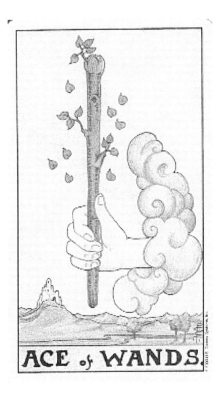

Keyword: Beginnings

Quick List:

Upright
- ♣ New beginnings
- ♣ Career changes
- ♣ New goals
- ♣ Fresh start
- ♣ Taking a new path
- ♣ Start of new projects

Reversed
- ♣ Job loss
- ♣ Lay off
- ♣ Firing
- ♣ Lying to get ahead
- ♣ False documentation

In-Depth:

Upright: Wands represent all the things that happen in your day-to-day life. For most of us, that means work issues. The Ace of Wands indicates new beginnings. Things will be changing in your work life very soon. You find yourself taking a new and unexpected path. Your career goals will be drastically altered. But all your goals seem to become clearer. Your everyday life enters new phases and you experience new adventures, new projects and a fresh start. There is a distinct possibility that you will get the job you have been seeking with all the perks and benefits that you were hoping to acquire.

Reversed: This is not a particularly good card for your reading. It can portend an imminent job loss. Your company will close or be sold and moved. You could get laid off due to downsizing. Getting fired, with or without cause is also a distinct possibility. It indicates that you are poorly prepared for the tasks at hand. It can also indicate that you have been lying about your abilities in order to gain a position. You have made false statements on your job application, or you have supplied fake documentation, such as altered birth certificates, falsified citizenship papers, lying about your education (forged degree) or falsely stating you have never been convicted of a crime. You could also be taking credit for someone else's work (plagiarism, etc.). Those types of dishonesties will likely catch up to you if the Ace is in the reversed position.

TWO OF WANDS

Keyword: Self-empowerment

Quick List:

Upright
- ♣ Empowerment
- ♣ Independence
- ♣ Achievement
- ♣ Personal success
- ♣ New ventures
- ♣ Peace

Reversed
- ♣ Business failure
- ♣ Downturn
- ♣ Inopportune time
- ♣ Rip-off by trusted partner

In-Depth:

Upright: A great card for your reading, the Two of Wands is about self-empowerment. The world is yours to navigate and your destiny is completely in your own hands. Turn your back on anyone who has power over you and take the leap of faith. Don't let other people or things hold you back. The time is ripe to find a new path. Striking out on your own will likely be a fortunate move. It is an opportune time to nurture your independent endeavors and find success in your business enterprises. Be at peace with your decisions. You have prepared adequately; success will follow. There are no hidden agendas indicated.

Reversed: Sometimes the time is not right for starting something new--the Two reversed says that time is now. Not only should you hold off on new ventures, but you should probably take measures to shore up the enterprises you are already involved in. The Two reversed portends business failure or collapse. You are in denial that there are serious problems afoot. Unfortunately, the Two also suggests that your downturn in business could be the result of an unscrupulous business partner. Watch you back and watch the cash drawer. It is likely your partner has a knife in one hand, and the other hand is in the till. Thieves are often known commodities and usually smile as they rob you blind. Stay alert.

THREE OF WANDS

Keyword: Satisfaction

Quick List:

Upright
- ♣ Satisfaction with self
- ♣ Anticipation of future
- ♣ Triumph
- ♣ Count your blessings
- ♣ Enjoying successes
- ♣ Planning for the next phase

Reversed
- ♣ Barrenness
- ♣ Un-achieved goals
- ♣ Change of plans
- ♣ Failure of ideas
- ♣ Needing help to achieve
- ♣ Unwarranted bragging

In-Depth:

Upright: The Three of Wands indicates that you feel satisfaction with all you oversee. Everything seems secure. Your accomplishments are in place and you are happy with where you are in life. There is contentment with where the journey has taken you. But you still are looking forward to what is coming in the future. You are planning the next phase and figuring out how to build on what you have. You have a solid foundation and are ready for whatever happens. Faith in yourself and your accomplishments is unwavering. You have chosen a path and plan to stay the course. It is a card of counting your blessings, and of being grateful for what you have. But it can also indicate that you are only looking forward on one path and are blinded to other things around you. Take the time to look in all directions and make sure you investigate all the options, even when you are secure with the path you have chosen.

Reversed: You weary of the journey, which has been a very tough road. Your goals have not been achieved and usually have fallen painfully short of what you anticipated. It is difficult to see your ideas fail and to find it necessary to change plans mid-stream, especially when you assumed that everything would go as planned. Worse yet, you are forced to admit that you can't do it on your own. You were not as prepared as you thought you were, and having to ask for help is stuck in your craw. There is a good chance that you rested on your laurels instead of doing what needed to be done. To make matters worse you bragged about it and are forced to eat crow. All you want now is the comfort of home.

FOUR OF WANDS

Keyword: Marriage

Quick List:

Upright	**Reversed**
♣ Marriage	♣ Relocation
♣ Celebration	♣ Home improvements
♣ Happy home-life	needed
♣ Joy	♣ Discord in the home
♣ Contentment	♣ Cancelled celebrations
♣ Being blessed	♣ Confusion

In-Depth:

Upright: The Four of Wands is a joyful card. It is the card of celebration. Most often used to portend a happy or upcoming marriage, it can also mean a wonderful celebration of such-- anniversary party or wedding reception or simply that you will soon be co-habitating with your significant other. It can mean a happy home, one filled with laughter and love or one about to be blessed by children. Family gatherings are also indicated. There is day-to-day joy in the household, an overall feeling of contentment in your life. You are ready for all the good things life has to offer. You could even move to a wonderful new house. The Four can also portend a happy homecoming, either for you finally coming home or the celebration of someone else coming home.

Reversed: There could be a change of location in your residence, perhaps even a cross country move, but it won't necessarily be by choice or cause any sense of happiness or contentment. Or you want a new home, but it just isn't going to happen now. The Four reversed also indicates the necessity for home improvements, as well as either routine maintenance or repair of damage from natural causes (weather related). It also means that there is an atmosphere of discord or tension in your home. You have lost the welcoming spirit to invite others into your home. There could be a cancellation of parties or other celebrations. A wedding might be postponed or called off entirely. A friendship ends. There is much confusion and lingering sadness when the Four is reversed, and your home is not a happy or comforting place to spend your time.

FIVE OF WANDS

Keyword: Conflict

Quick List:

Upright
- ♣ Surrounded by conflict
- ♣ Being in the middle
- ♣ Backbiting
- ♣ Tension at work
- ♣ Competition vs. cooperation

Reversed
- ♣ Taking the neutral stance
- ♣ Removing yourself from situation
- ♣ Agitating person leaves
- ♣ Conflict ends
- ♣ Negative situation abates

In-Depth:

Upright: You are surrounded by conflict, many times it is conflict of unknown direction or indistinct aim. Perhaps you find yourself in the middle of someone else's argument. There is backbiting in a community situation, in a town meeting, at the office or in an organizational group. Tension in the atmosphere is palpable. Someone in the group is not a team player. He asks for your help and then turns on you after the fact. You can't tell if a person is telling you the truth or is just being sarcastic in their commentary. There is definitely an agitator in the group causing much disruption from the norm. The Five of Wands can also indicate that there is a feeling of unhealthy competition where there should be an air of cooperation.

Reversed: The Five reversed indicates resolution of problems. A negative situation is put to rest in the work place. The person causing the conflict is removed from the situation, and miraculously the problems disappear along with the agitator. On the other hand, you could remove yourself from the situation completely, or you take yourself out of play and retreat to a neutral corner. One way or another, the conflict ends.

SIX OF WANDS

Keyword: Victory

Quick List:

Upright
- ♣ Laurels
- ♣ Victory
- ♣ Promotion
- ♣ New job
- ♣ Accomplishments
- ♣ Good reputation

Reversed
- ♣ Lack of assertiveness
- ♣ Loss of regard
- ♣ Self-sabotage
- ♣ Overlooked for promotion
- ♣ No recognition

In-Depth:

Upright: The Six of Wands symbolizes victory and success. Recognized for your accomplishments, you are finally given your due. That promotion or new job is forthcoming and is based on your ability, work record and work ethic. You are in control. Everything you plan is coming to fruition. All of your co-workers wish you well. They consider you a leader, a good person, and they think highly of you. It is your turn to take the victory lap. But you never wallow in the victory. Hard work is what put you in this position and it is what you return to after the applause.

Reversed: It is hard enough when you don't live up to the expectations of others, but the Six reversed indicates you fail to live up to your own expectations as well. Sometimes you are your own worst enemy, sabotaging yourself in the workplace, even allowing others to take credit for your achievements. You lack the assertiveness required to stand up for yourself, either through low self esteem or fear of reprisal. You are definitely not a ladder climber, but being self-effacing only has you being overlooked for promotion. It is time to take stock of how you view yourself and how others view you at work. Be honest with yourself and develop a plan to be more assertive. If you have a firm belief in yourself, soon others will hold you in high esteem.

SEVEN OF WANDS

Keyword: Unseen Opposition

Quick List:

Upright	**Reversed**
♣ Unseen enemy	♣ No opposition
♣ Be cautious	♣ Obstacles removed
♣ Unexpected problems	♣ Ease of accomplishment
♣ Opposition to plans	♣ Cakewalk
♣ One thing after another	♣ Calm, steady flow

In-Depth:

Upright: Somehow, no matter what you do, nothing seems to go as planned. It is almost as if someone is out there, thwarting your every effort. The Seven of Wands indicates that there are indeed forces operating at odds with your desires. But it is a problem if you are not sure what or whom you are fighting against. It could just be a state of bad karma, the wheel coming back around as payback for something you did in the past. You also feel that there are secrets working against you, information you know would help the situation but cannot seem to access despite your best efforts. On the other hand, there could be open opposition to your plans that comes from left field or from an unexpected source. Regardless, it seems that your luck is not with you as one thing after another conflicts with and delays the desired outcome. There are decisions to be made and you are finding it difficult to choose the right path. You are vulnerable. Be cautious.

Reversed: Things are going well. With the Seven reversed, you are taking a cakewalk. There are no obstacles in your path; there is no opposition. If you remain on your present course, you will arrive at your destination with no unforeseen delays. It is a time of good charm. You have a firm grip on things. Go for it.

EIGHT OF WANDS

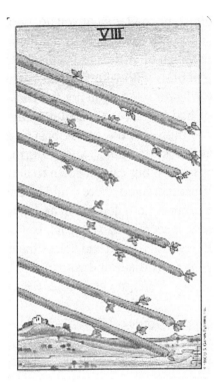

Keyword: Communication

Quick List:

Upright
- ♣ Movement
- ♣ Communications
- ♣ Travel
- ♣ Media coverage
- ♣ Ease of plans
- ♣ Dreams come true

Reversed
- ♣ Jealousy
- ♣ Cancellation of travel
- ♣ Disruption of plans
- ♣ Failure of ideas
- ♣ Hardship

In-Depth:

Upright: The Eight of Wands is a positive card. It indicates voluntary movement, as in vacations. You are in for a long flight, perhaps travel abroad. Speaking of long flights, an astronaut scheduled for a shuttle flight might see this card in a reading. Your plans will fall in place for that trip you have longed to take. It is a dream coming to fruition. All good things find their way to you at this time. It also indicates communication in all its forms. You might become the object of media coverage, be it in the newspaper, on radio or on television. One way or another, you find yourself in the spotlight. With the positive energies of the Eight, your time before the camera will result in good coverage, not negative scandal pieces. You could be involved in extensive, upbeat communications by mail, phone or via the Internet. Don't discount the possibility of engaging in an on-line affair. High tech communications could also indicate your use of global positioning equipment or even chip implants in your pets.

Reversed: That trip you have scheduled is likely to be canceled if the Eight reversed shows up in the reading. If you are thinking about taking a trip, it would be wise to reconsider the plan. There will definitely be a disruption of your agenda. Things are generally skewed; if there are problems at this time, they could be the result of jealousy. Failure of your ideas, meetings that fall through and general work hardships can also be due to a jealous person in your life.

NINE OF WANDS

Keyword: Holding On

Quick List:

Upright
- ♣ Holding on to things
- ♣ Hurt but undecided
- ♣ Fearful of loss
- ♣ Bound by fear
- ♣ Self-imposed restriction
- ♣ Stagnation

Reversed
- ♣ Un-fearful
- ♣ Freedom
- ♣ Adventurous
- ♣ Growth

In-Depth:

Upright: The Nine of Wands indicates that you have many things, but you are so fearful of losing them, that you spend all your time clinging to what you have. You are fearful of being without the things you have earned, and you are afraid to lose the security those things provide. This could be material goods, family, friends or your employment. You fear taking risks because you are afraid to get hurt. This leaves you in a constant state of stagnation; not going forward, not going back. There is no growth of person or character because you are completely self-involved. You are looking for a way out but you fear taking the leap of faith. When you do move forward, you take the pieces of the past, good or bad, with you.

Reverse: The time has come to free yourself from the restriction of self-involvement. You are able to reach out to new people and toward new goals. New adventures become a thing to anticipate with joy, rather than fear. It is a time of great personal growth. Take the leap. Learn something new, take a class, learn to play the piano. Free yourself from the self-imposed bondage of fear of the unknown. Remember, even if you lose a little, you gain enormously in the effort.

TEN OF WANDS

Keyword: Burden

Quick List:

Upright	Reversed
♣ Bearing other's burdens	♣ Tough love
♣ Control issues	♣ Saying no
♣ Super-mom syndrome	♣ Not becoming a doormat
♣ Taking on too much	♣ Avoiding responsibility
♣ Never saying no	♣ Not carrying your share of
♣ Striving for sainthood	the load

In-Depth:

Upright: The Ten of Wands says you are a glutton for punishment. You are constantly shouldering the burdens of others and taking on their responsibilities as your own. Some would call you a control freak and they would be correct in that assessment. You are everything to everyone and feed on other people saying and thinking you are wonderful because you can handle and accomplish so much. If you are female, you often suffer from Super-Mom Syndrome, working full-time, chauffeuring the kids, taking on most of the household responsibilities, being the perfect hostess, chairing the PTA and on and on *ad nauseum*. Or you just have a martyr complex, feeling you "have" to do everything in order for things to be done right.

Reverse: It is time for some major tough love. If your child keeps coming to you to solve financial problems, is loafing around, is unemployed and living at home, it's time to give them the big boot. All those around you should be forced to carry their own burdens. Stop letting everyone dump on you, mentally or physically. But the Ten reversed can also mean that you are the one who refuses to accept responsibility, and you are running away from the things you should be doing. You want and expect others to carry your burdens. Buck up and pull your own weight! People with problems of their own should not be expected to shoulder your baggage as well.

Section 3:

THE MAJOR ARCANA

INTRODUCTION TO THE MAJOR ARCANA

The cards of the Major Arcana represent the endless journey of the soul. The Major cards refer to the journey of the soul as it has been affected by its past life, its present situation and possible future paths.

In a typical spread, look to the Major Arcana as most important, because the depth of these cards directly affects the current situation. The classical interpretations of the Major cards still hold true. The guidelines for these cards have been set for centuries.

When the cards of the Major Arcana are reversed they indicate that we do not recognize these traits in ourselves, or that the direct opposite of the upright meaning is happening (unless otherwise specified).

The following poem is an easy and quick way to remember the Major cards. Once you learn it, you will never forget the meanings of these indicators of the soul's journey.

Prepare for what you're about to do
Allow your subconscious to guide you through. **Fool**
Love and money, work and power
Are the tools you need to make changes flower. **Magician**
Mysteries have yet to be revealed
Prepare to learn; use what you feel. **High Priestess**
Ideas are fertile, and all you ask for
Are guidance and wisdom-that's it, nothing more.
Empress, Emperor
Courage to lead will help you choose. **Heirophant**

But think long and deep; the choices belong to you. **Lovers**
Prepare yourself to fight the fight
Victory comes with the morning light. **Chariot**
Don't be afraid to continue on
You've planned it well; your mind is strong. **Strength**
Now you begin to see the light
The path's not dark--it's very light. **The Hermit**
The gods of fortune smile down on you
Things fall into place; as they're meant to do.
Wheel of Fortune
Justice prevails, rewards for your labor
Legal things are in your favor. **Justice**
Things seem stagnant, but just for today.
Keep on believing; persistence will pay. **Hanged Man**
The transition comes--so don't be frightened
These changes will make your soul enlightened. **Death**
Moderate and patient be
Time and fortitude are the keys. **Temperance**
Look to what you think and do
Your own worst enemy is you. **The Devil**
Things may change from what you planned
Turmoil disguises the light that's at hand. **The Tower**
You've fulfilled your dream, your wishes come true
Wisdom and happiness follow you.
The Star, The Moon, The Sun
You've done a good job, you are judged well done
But remember the journey is a continuing one. **Judgement**
Now the journey is complete
The answer's been given, the world's at your feet. **The World**

THE FOOL

The Fool is Number 0 in the Tarot deck. It is neither the beginning nor the end, and represents the endless cycles of the soul's journey.

Keyword: Prepare

Quick List:

	Upright	**Reversed**
	New venture	Not prepared
	Alternate path	Delay

In-Depth:

Upright: The Fool is neither the beginning nor the end. It is the cycles of life. As each cycle ends another begins. The Fool symbolizes the soul's journey. Be prepared for whatever comes next. You may be getting married, or suddenly discover that you are an unknown person inside who was waiting for the right time to emerge. The Fool's purpose is to make you aware that it is much more expedient to be prepared for the journey and not step foolishly into new situations without preparation. Listen to your inner voice. The Fool does not discourage taking risks. It challenges us not to take foolish risks. Don't become so arrogant to think that you know everything.

Reversed: This is not a good time to begin a new venture. It will be cancelled or delayed because you are not prepared. You need more education, more money and more power to begin. Rethink all plans carefully before embarking on the journey.

THE MAGICIAN

THE MAGICIAN.

The Magician is Number 1 in the Tarot deck. It represents the manifestation of change.

Keyword: Change

Quick List:

	Upright	Reversed
∞	Use your power	Not ready for change
	Make it happen	Being blocked

In-Depth:

Upright: The Magician is the manifestation of change. This comes about using the tools of the Tarot, which are love, money, power and work. Change is inevitable, so you might as well go with the flow, because there's a major change coming your way. The Magician is a card of motivation and organization. We have and will always have our own empowerment and motivation. This has been and will always be the key to any major life change. But consider the tools we now have to create the future. With the constant advances in science and technologies, we no longer have any excuses for not manifesting change. The Magician is truly a motivating, inspiring card, telling you to move ahead, to take charge of your new plans and offering hope in all you attempt.

Reversed: You don't have what is required at this time to make a significant change in your life. Negative thoughts are blocking you from new beginnings. It is difficult to be successful at a new venture when you don't possess the tools necessary to accomplish the goal. Prepare yourself.

The High Priestess is the Number 2 card in the Tarot deck and represents the essence of the feminine.

Keyword: The Feminine Principle

Quick List:		
	Upright	**Reversed**
	Feminine intuition	Secrets
	Sexuality	Low self-esteem

In-Depth:

Upright: Using intuitive abilities, you are regarded as a wise person who is spiritually, physically and mentally gifted. You rely on what you have learned from previous journeys, drawing on knowledge deep within your subconscious. The High Priestess is the essence of everything feminine. She is the Yin, and represents sexuality. In a reading, the High Priestess can mean that you will find the perfect mate, or that the relationship your are in is overflowing with dynamic sexual chemistry. The physical side of your relationship is very strong. But it can also indicate feminine vanity. This is the card of tummy tucks, tattooed eyebrows and eyeliner, botox injections and eye-lifts.

Reversed: There are things regarding a person you love and trust that are yet to be discovered. The High Priestess reversed can indicate an affair on the part of your partner. Sex between you and your partner is not good or no longer as good as it used to be. In some cases, sex is used as a tool to manipulate or punish. You could be suffering from a bad case of low self-esteem. There is a possibility of minor difficulties regarding the reproductive organs, such as hormonal imbalance. There is also a risk of contracting or passing on a sexually transmitted disease, especially if the High Priestess appears in the reading in conjunction with many cards from the suit of Swords.

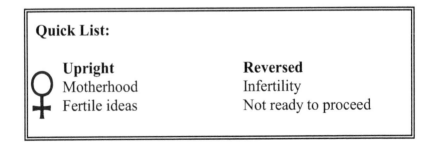

The Empress is the Number 3 in the Tarot deck. She represents fertility in all its forms, personal and business.

Keyword: Fertility

Quick List:

	Upright	Reversed
	Motherhood	Infertility
	Fertile ideas	Not ready to proceed

In-Depth:

Upright: The Empress is the Mother of all things. All endeavors are fertile and fruitful at this time. If you are wondering about pregnancy, this card would indicate the time is ripe. If you are trying to become pregnant, the Empress portends that it will come to pass, but it may be through in-vitro fertilization, donor eggs, artificial insemination, hormone therapy or even adoption. It is a time to use what you know and take all that you have prepared yourself to do to reach the desired goals. Giving birth to new ideas is common now. Everything holds the promises of womanhood, nurturing, maturing and growing.

Reversed: There is difficulty in conceiving a child. A pregnancy could be interrupted by miscarriage or abortion. There could be problems with a pregnancy (determined by surrounding cards). The Empress reversed also indicates menopause if found with the High Priestess and the Three of Swords. It is a time of tribulation with female authority figures. There is careless planning on your part. Go back over the details to prevent the project from unraveling.

THE EMPEROR

The Emperor is Number 4 in the Tarot deck and represents all manner of authority.

Keyword: Authority

Quick List::

Upright	Reversed
Fatherhood	Immaturity
Lessons	Mental weakness

In-Depth:

Upright: The Emperor is the Father figure, the authority figure and a very accomplished male. His authority is achieved by wisdom and experience. That experience can be from the conscious present or from the subconscious. In the upright position, the Emperor is used to determine the question of fatherhood. It can indicate that you will become a parent in the present or future or that you will acquire a male authority figure (e.g., mother remarries). It also indicates lessons you remember learning from your parents. When found in a reading near cards from the suit of Swords, you should research your genetic links to diseases such as heart problems, high blood pressure, diabetes and a host of other genetic time bombs. It can indicate that you need to seek advice from an older and wiser soul.

Reversed: You question parentage, but the answer is doubtful or not at all what you anticipate. You take umbrage with male authority figures. The Emperor reversed can also indicate a deceased male authority figure such as a father or grandfather. There is a lack of maturity in your thinking. You need to grow up and get a clue.

THE HEIROPHANT

The Hierophant is the Number 5 in the Tarot deck. He is the counselor, representing the wisdom of the ages.

Keyword: Wisdom

Quick List:

	Upright	**Reversed**
	Tradition	Nontraditional methods
	Advice	Flexibility

236

In-Depth:

Upright: The Hierophant is the wise counselor. He represents the traditional tried and true ways of doing things. You have inner knowledge of what is right and wrong, gained from past experience, and should use it now to resolve any problems. Others see you as established and entrenched in your belief systems. It is difficult for you to deviate from what feels comfortable and right. It is not the time for you to take risks; stick with what you know will work. You are wise enough to be at ease in seeking or dispensing educated advice. But your knowledge is more than just an educated guess. You have the wisdom of the ages in your subconscious to use as needed.

Reversed: You become the opposite of all that is traditional using non-traditional methods and alternative solutions to everything. You might choose a totally unlikely partner in life or business. It is likely that you will seek non-traditional methods of medical treatment such as acupuncture, reiki, reflexology, holistic healers and meditation. Stepping outside the box, you find extremely creative ways to make money. You are innovative in your thinking, inventing cutting-edge products or coming up with unheard of solutions but always using an alternative route to reach the goal. Seeking guidance through oracles is right up your alley. But you could also be an inveterate dreamer, living a life grounded in fantasy.

THE LOVERS

The Lovers are Number 6 in the Tarot deck and represent the paths of choice.

Keyword: Choice

Quick List:

Upright	Reversed
Good relationships	Poor choices
Healing	Poor relationships

In-Depth:

Upright: The Lovers indicate there are choices to be made. It is time to choose what is right for you, be it regarding a relationship, a career change or any other important choice. The Archangel Raphael, depicted on this card, suggests that you will find a time, a place or a person to help heal what has been destroyed in the past. You may meet a new love that will be a turning point in your life. Or an exciting new job may become available after months of searching. There will be choices regarding friends and relationships and you will make the appropriate choices. The Lovers portend the beginning of new relationships.

Reversed: You are involved in a love relationship that is unhealthy. Your current love may be demeaning, mentally or verbally abusive, taking away from what is good for your heart and soul. When the Lovers are reversed there is little if any love surrounding you. It can be a card of hopelessness and poor choices. Be careful and do your homework before you make choices at this time.

The Chariot is Number 7 in the Tarot deck and represents victory after a struggle.

Keyword: Victory

Quick List:

	Upright	**Reversed**
	Achievement	Losses
	Recognition	Struggle

In-Depth:

Upright: The Chariot is the card of victory. You have fought a hard battle, but your courage and tenacity have held you in good stead. There is recognition for a job well done and your achievements are lauded and applauded by others. You have moved and continue to move forward despite all obstacles, and you will succeed in spite of those difficulties. The Chariot means the realization of long-held dreams, such as completing that novel you always wanted to write or finishing your first marathon run. Success is on your horizon. The Chariot is also used to depict travel or purchase of a new vehicle. The vehicle can be an automobile or a motorcycle, but taken in the spiritual sense, the vehicle is all that you have learned in life speeding you to the next step. It is a joyous victory, but don't let it go to your head. Keep control of your emotions.

Reversed: You are just not winning the game when the Chariot is reversed. It is impossible to achieve power at the present. Your struggles result in frustration rather than victory. Use caution when driving any vehicles. Keep a low profile.

Strength is the Number 8 in the Tarot deck and depicts courage frosted with humanity.

Keyword: Courage

Quick List:

	Upright	Reversed
	Don't be afraid	Be cautious
	Take risks	Remain at a standstill

242

In-Depth:

Upright: Do not be afraid. When Strength is upright, you have the courage to meet all problems head on. But you are not malevolent in confrontation. Love, gentleness and kindness are often the tools you use to win over, or overcome, your enemies. Your spirituality conquers the negative energies of those around you. Believe deeply in what you know to be true. Don't back down from the fiercest challenge. Good will triumph over evil. Instinctively you know that love is more important than gaining material things. The power of the universe, portrayed by the symbol of infinite wisdom on the Strength card, defines this truth: what has always been the right thing to do will always be the right thing. You will be required to be strong for those you love.

Reversed: It is not a good time to be fearless. Use caution. Don't be rash in your actions or judgements. It is time to let other people help. Lean on others.

THE HERMIT

The Hermit is Number 9 in the Tarot deck and represents the light of divine guidance.

Keyword: Light

Quick List:

Upright	**Reversed**
Light at the end of the tunnel	No end in sight
New forces become apparent	Loneliness

In-Depth:

Upright: The Hermit carries the light, leading the way through the darkness. It is the light that shines through your heart. As he lights the path ahead, he shows the way to find the answers to your questions. You carry the light within yourself, and the answers have always been there, but the Hermit will help you dig deep and find them. If you take some time to separate yourself from the problem and ponder the solution, it will come to you. Regardless of the problem, there is light at the end of the tunnel. When the hermit appears, do not hesitate to seek advice and guidance, but ultimately, the decision is yours alone to make. Do what feels right.

Reversed: Although you seek the light, you may not recognize it when the Hermit is reversed. But don't worry, help is on the way. You might feel alone, yet you are not. The power of the Supreme Being and the power of the universe is there. Don't forget to seek that divine intervention in your unhappiness.

THE WHEEL OF FORTUNE

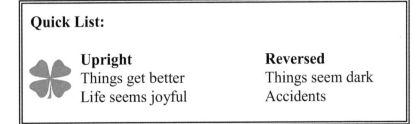

WHEEL of FORTUNE.

The Wheel of Fortune is Number 10 in the Tarot deck and represents luck and opportunity.

Keyword: Luck

Quick List:

	Upright	Reversed
	Things get better	Things seem dark
	Life seems joyful	Accidents

In-Depth:

Upright: The Wheel of Fortune is the card everyone wants to see in their reading. The universe is bringing your life into an upwardly moving cycle. There seems to be endless opportunities, and everything you touch turns to gold. Don't be afraid to take risks. Now is the time to make changes in careers and financial ventures. If there was ever a time to gamble, this is it. Buy that lottery ticket or bet on that high-paying long shot. High-risk investments are not as "iffy" as they sound. It is a good bet that the risky path holds promise. There will be a good outcome.

Reversed: Things seem to be spiraling downward and they just might be, but the gods of fortune carry the wheel upward. Don't lose hope, just know that in time it will be alright. Now is not the time to waste money on gambling; you will be throwing good money after bad. This is not a good time to take risks.

JUSTICE

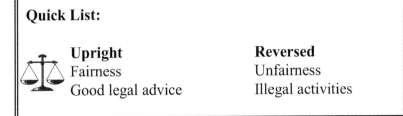

Justice is Number 11 in the Tarot deck and represents fairness and balance.

Keyword: Balance

Quick List:

	Upright	**Reversed**
	Fairness	Unfairness
	Good legal advice	Illegal activities

In-Depth:

Upright: The Justice card brings fairness and balance. Legal judgements are in your favor. If you are being judged, you will be judged fairly. You will win the lawsuit, be compensated fairly in the divorce, or win custody of a child. Any legal question will be settled to your satisfaction. Decisions and choices you make at this time in your life are well thought out and ring true and right. With this card, you can also see the balance of life; what goes around, comes around. It could also indicate that you are, or should be, following a career path into the legal profession. You could be a first rate lawyer, policeman, probation officer or other related job. Your sense of fairness from past lives or experiences makes you very adept at this sort of career.

Reversed: Legal matters are not in your favor. You feel that you are treated unfairly in some situations, but you are not objective. Are you following the rules? If not, this would be the time to look over your shoulder. Don't flaunt the law. Justice reversed indicates an unfavorable outcome in a lawsuit. Criminal activity will get you some jail time. You will be caught so STOP NOW. You are the object of racial or other discrimination.

THE HANGED MAN

The Hanged Man is Number 12 in the Tarot deck and represents stagnation.

Keyword: Stagnation

Quick List:

Upright	Reversed
Project at a standstill	Things move quickly
Boredom	New way of thinking

In-Depth:

Upright: When the Hanged Man appears, everything seems to be in a state of stagnation. Try though you might, you will only spin your wheels and go nowhere. This situation should be viewed as temporary. Inevitably things will begin to move again. Often the stagnation abates with the arrival of a surprising development. You are overly anxious or unable to see that a situation is not in your best interest. Step back and analyze why things have come to a screeching halt. Reach deep inside to see what action can be taken to reverse the state of stagnation that surrounds you.

Reversed: It is not the time for new projects. Forcing things will not be profitable. Wait until things are moving before implementing new ideas. Only the universe can give you a jumpstart.

DEATH

Death is Number 13 in the Tarot deck and represents life's transitions.

Keyword: Transition

Quick List:

	Upright	**Reversed**
	Major change	Not a good transformation
	Controlled change	Uncontrolled change

In-Depth:

Upright: Contrary to popular belief, the Death card does not mean physical death. Rather it depicts a major transition in your life. To be qualified as a Death card, the situation must contain the four major elements as depicted by the Minor Arcana of the Tarot. It must affect your day-to-day living, your personal relationships, your financial situation and your personal empowerment. These types of transition events are the same ones most often associated with the highest stress situations. They include entering the work force after completing your education, marriage, divorce, having children, the children growing up and leaving home, going back to school, moving across the country, changing careers, inheriting or winning an extremely large amount of money, or losing a significant amount of money. Be aware that you do have control over these situations. It is unlikely that the Death card will appear in the reading of a person who is very secure in their life at the moment. Interestingly, while the Death card may seem frightening to those who are uncomfortable with change, it always results in a comfortable conclusion. There is renewal at all levels with the Death card.

Reversed: The Death card reversed often means that things have come to a halt and no major changes are forthcoming. But sometimes a reversed Death card indicates that an event over which you have absolutely no control will change your life. These include job loss due to corporate downsizing, a company bankruptcy causing the loss of your pension, a spouse just walks away from a marriage without a good reason, or an illness that forces you to move from your home to a more manageable place. Most of these things will appear with just enough warning to give you time to prepare.

TEMPERANCE

Temperance is Number 14 in the Tarot deck and represents moderation in all things.

Keyword: Moderation

Quick List:	
Upright	**Reversed**
Prudence	Indiscretion
Moderateness	Recklessness

254

In-Depth:

Upright: The Archangel Uriel, depicted on the Temperance card, cautions you to practice moderation in all things. Maintain the status quo. Keep doing things carefully and thoughtfully. It is good to practice restraint and keep things on an even keel. Nurture yourself carefully and in a well-balanced manner, physically, mentally, emotionally and spiritually. Take time to relax and balance out your fast-moving, high-stress work life. Live well. Be calm and serene in the knowledge that the powers of the universe are ebbing and flowing as they should.

Reversed: Be cautious. You have a tendency to make irrational judgements at this time. You do too much, too fast and too soon. Take the time to list the pros and cons of a situation, or you run the risk of doing something rash.

THE DEVIL

The Devil is Number 15 in the Tarot deck and represents all forms of bondage.

Keyword: Bondage

Quick List:

Upright	**Reversed**
Negative thoughts	Release
Prisoner of poor choices	Positivity

In-Depth:

Upright: The Devil is not so much an evil card as it is a negative one. It represents the prisons that you make for yourself. You allow negative emotion to hold you hostage, preventing your own growth as a human being. It is a good time to look at how you feel and analyze why you feel that way, because you're allowing negativity to guide your life. Anxiety, greed and resentment; jealousy, fear, dishonesty and duplicity have become the mainstays of your daily living. Above all, these attitudes hurt you much more than they hurt anyone else. Your moral compass is spinning wildly as you seek a way out of this mind-set on a subconscious level. The Devil also indicates addictions that are holding you in bondage. These addictions take different forms, be it a tendency to form bad relationships or physical addictions as in drug use or alcohol abuse. The Devil is fueled by the very things that make you human and serves as a reminder to examine your frailties.

Reversed: You release the things that are holding you back and move forward. You seek treatment for addictions and turn over a new page in the book of your life.

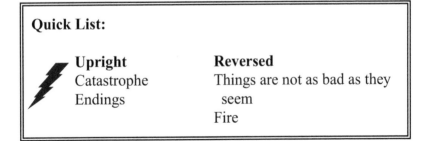

The Tower is Number 16 in the Tarot and portends chaos.

Keyword: Chaos

Quick List:

	Upright	Reversed
⚡	Catastrophe	Things are not as bad as they
	Endings	seem
		Fire

In-Depth:

Upright: The Tower is the card of inescapable and often times sudden change. It depicts total chaos as opposed to the life we have become comfortable living. It is the proverbial bolt out of the blue that changes everything in an instant. But be it a natural disaster, an illness, a broken relationship or even a serious lifestyle curtailment, the Tower still carries a message of hope: Good will come from the bad. It is interesting to correlate the Tower card that has evolved through the centuries to present day events, such as the World Trade Tower disaster on September 11. As the card depicts, there was destruction of a physically existing tower that changed the lives of many people. But amidst the tragedy, our citizens found a new unity and love for country and mankind. The heroism and bravery of many, renewed our hope in humanity.

Reversed: Things are not as bad as they seem. Hang onto your hopes and eventually things will work out. Your worst fears are not realized.

THE STAR

The Star is Number 17 in the Tarot deck and represents our hopes and wishes.

Keyword: Wishes

Quick List:

Upright
Dreams come true
Get what you wish for

Reversed
Wish not fulfilled
Forgetting to be positive

In-Depth:

Upright: The Star is the card of wish fulfillment. The plans and dreams you have been working on are being realized. Simply put, what you wish for will be yours when the card is in the upright position.

Reversed: Your wishes will not be granted at this time. When the Star is reversed it is more expedient to spend your energy seeing to other's needs and desires.

The Moon is Number 18 in the Tarot deck and represents intuition.

Keyword: Intuition

Quick List:		
	Upright	**Reversed**
	Psychic energy	Not listening to inner voice
	Intuition	The Force is not with you

In-Depth:

Upright: The Moon is the card of intuition, precognition and psychic energy. You just know something for no apparent reason. Listen to your inner voice for guidance. Now is the time when you need to rely on those feelings and hunches.

Reversed: Your intuition could be faulty right now, or you could be persisting in doing things counter to what you intuitively know is right. Both of these situations will produce unwanted results. Think twice about proceeding and go with your gut feeling.

The Sun is Number 19 in the Tarot deck and represents joy and happiness.

Keyword: Happiness

Quick List:

	Upright	Reversed
	Joy	Clouds over your happiness
	Happiness	Worry

In-Depth:

Upright: When the Sun is upright, be prepared for abundant joy and happiness. Good things are coming to you. All endeavors are blessed. In regard to specific questions, the upright Sun is a positive response.

Reversed: There are clouds over your happiness. Usually this is due to problems with someone you love. You are worrying excessively. Learn to take the bumps in the road, but give them only as much concern as is necessary.

Judgement is Number 20 in the Tarot deck and represents how we judge or how we are judged.

Keyword: How we are seen

Quick List:		
	Upright	**Reversed**
	Reward	Poor judgement
	Favorable judgement	Must defend yourself

In-Depth:

Upright: You have led your life well and positive things come your way when the Judgement card is upright in the reading. Your judgement is good and you are rewarded. If involved in any litigation, the judgement will be favorable toward you. Your judgement of character is right on the money.

Reversed: Stop using poor judgement. Rethink the situation and start again. Relying on faulty judgement will only lead down the wrong path. This card reversed can also mean that you are being misjudged by someone else. Be prepared to defend your position.

THE WORLD

The World is Number 21 in the Tarot deck and represents completion.

Keyword: Completion

Quick List:

	Upright	**Reversed**
	Completion	Cycle not complete
	Things to come	Your world is shaky

In-Depth:

Upright: Everything comes together now when the World is upright. All that you have attempted is complete and fruitful. This cycle of your life is ending, bringing you back to the Fool and enabling a new cycle to begin. You finally got that degree, or the kids have left the nest, or the divorce is final and you are ready to start again. You feel the sense of completion.

Reversed: Your world seems shaky. The present cycle of your life is not complete. Be patient and keep moving forward. It's not over yet. Perhaps you feel that you are finished at a career, relationship or project. Suddenly you find you're not finished at all. It is only a temporary stall in the cycle.

Section 4:

ALL THE REST

READING AND LAYOUTS

* Talk to your querent and select a significator card (court card) to represent the querent in the reading.
* Shuffle the deck many times. Make sure the cards are turned in both directions throughout the deck.
* Hand the deck to the querent.
* The querent should shuffle the deck thoroughly while asking the questions that need to be answered.
* Take the cards and lay out the spread, once for each question and one question at a time.
* When you lay out the cards, turn them over like the pages in a book. Don't flip the cards end over end because that changes the aspect of the card in the reading. It is necessary to lay them in the same position they have in the shuffled deck; therefore they should be turned like book pages.
* Upright is upright to you, the reader. Reversed is reversed to you, the reader.
* A crossing card in the Celtic Cross spread is always read as an upright card.

There are three simple spreads you can master easily as you learn to read the Tarot. The first is the three-card spread, shown below.

THE THREE-CARD SPREAD

The querent asks a question. The first card turned represents the question. The middle card represents the action that should or could be taken. The last card turned is the outcome likely if the action is taken. As the querent continues to ask questions, you continue to set out three cards per question, working from the top of the deck. Do not reuse the cards that have already been placed.

THE 12-MONTH SPREAD

Another simple spread to read is the 12-month spread. The cards are placed in the following way.

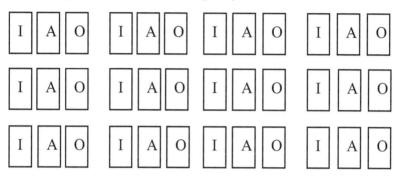

Each set of three cards represents a month of the year, starting with next month (the month after the reading). There are no questions to be asked. The reading is informational. It indicates the issue (I) of that month, the action (A) and the outcome (O) in a similar manner as the three-card spread. It gives the querent an overall view of the year to come.

THE CELTIC CROSS

The third layout is the Celtic cross. The cards are placed in the following fashion.

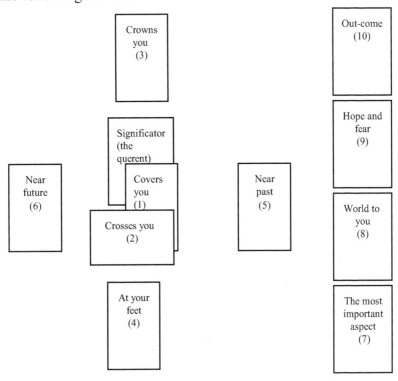

The significator is placed first, then the cards are dealt from the top of the deck according to the numbers indicated in the layout above. The card's first position is what covers you; it is the issue at hand. The second position is what crosses you; it identifies an obstacle or vehicle regarding the issue. The third position is what crowns you; it defines the way your thoughts indicate that you want the situation to progress. The fourth position is what you stand on; it encompasses all the mental, physical and spiritual events that have led to the situation. The fifth position is the near past; it reminds you of what has recently occurred that has affected the situation. The sixth position is the near future; it predicts what will soon occur to guide you to the outcome. The seventh position indicates why the issue is so important, either karmically or presently. The eighth position indicates how others can affect the situation. The ninth position indicates hopes and fears; what you hope will happen and what you fear may not. The tenth position is the outcome; it is the answer to the question.

TIPS FOR THE READER

The Tarot is an oracle that will tell you the direction your life is likely to take in any given situation. It will also give you options that will allow you to change the outcome. Always remember that free will is the strongest force in the universe; even stronger than the cards. You alone control your life. The Tarot is an informational tool that will help you become attuned and enlightened to forces within you and those surrounding you.

Explain to your querent that all things in life are guided by the will. If things appear difficult in a reading, look for alternative paths or answers as guided by the Tarot. The Tarot will not provide only one answer; it gives you alternate choices.

To truly maximize the information in the reading, the querent should be encouraged to ask specific questions. The card reader will determine the querent's answers based on how the cards fall. Most readers will pay careful attention to the degree of importance the querent assigns to his questions. Take note of the following helpful hints.

* Be objective. Don't let your relationship with the querent color what you say.
* Never let your opinion interfere with, or influence, your intuition.
* Don't say what you think a person WANTS to hear, simply interpret the cards.
* It is your obligation to tell the querent exactly what the cards say, even if the answer that appears in the reading is not what YOU think it should be.
* Delivery is everything. Always be gentle and compassionate in your approach, especially when the cards give a message that is difficult for the querent to hear.
* Don't forget, even if the news is not good, the cards will always give a solution, suggestion or an alternate path.

* The Tarot is meant to ENLIGHTEN, not to tell you what to do or make decisions for you.

As a responsible reader, you must be prepared to guide your clients toward help when necessary. Remember that you are a reader, not a psychologist. Many times you will encounter people who are very troubled, even suicidal, when they come to you for a reading. If this happens to you, be very empathetic, and provide the name and number of a good psychologist or a hotline. You will soon notice that when you are reading their cards, people will talk about everything and ask you anything! I keep many referrals on hand from psychologists, counselors and employment agencies, as well as government programs for job training, how to seek financial aid for education, contact numbers for agencies that supply help for the elderly and free prescription programs. I also have business cards from astrologers, artists, handymen, lawyers and a myriad of other professions that I can hand to clients who need help.

Compassion is critical. Although many seek the Tarot as a lark, you will find an extraordinary number of people who use the cards as an enlightening guide to daily problems and questions. It is immoral and irresponsible to take advantage of a person's vulnerability. There are ethics involved in reading the Tarot-- ethics that come with spirituality and common sense. When a person approaches you for a reading, give them just that, a reading. As a reader, offering additional services for a price, such as candle burning, lucky amulets and magic spells is spurious at best. It is absolutely essential that you honor and keep a person's information confidential. You will learn many things about people as you read for them. Keep all information to yourself. You have been given a great gift if you are able to intuit the Tarot. Don't be disrespectful of the cards, or of yourself, by using the Tarot for any reason other than the one for which it was created: to give enlightenment and hope to others.

When you are reading the Tarot, you have a great deal of

power. Your client is looking to you to interpret the cards and give him direction. Many unconscionable people will use the Tarot to advance themselves financially by talking you into more and more readings or charging very high prices. Only in a very traumatic situation should you consider reading the cards as frequently as one-month increments. This is done only to bolster your client's confidence and to help them mentally through a particularly bad time. Under normal circumstances, I would suggest not reading for a client more often than every three months, and generally I recommend six months between readings. And most people, if given a thorough and accurate reading, will choose to follow that recommendation. In order for events to come to pass, time must also pass. If a client is sitting at your table having readings more often than recommended, they are so busy trying to find clues to the future that they have no time or energy to actually move toward the future by day-to-day living.

The fees you charge, if indeed you do have a set fee, must be reasonable. Keep in mind that most people who come to you are looking for clarification of their own issues. They would not be there if they didn't need help. Also remember that we are all just normal working people. Take into account your God given gift, the fact that you must make a living and the type of people who seek you. A reasonable fee is between $30-$50 per reading. I firmly believe that readers who charge hundreds of dollars to help people along life's path are committing a serious abuse of power. We need one another's gifts to make life progress smoothly. Why be greedy?

My own personal standard is to never accept money from a person who is in a serious grief situation, such as the loss of a child. I never accept money from a person who is financially devastated or from men and women in the active military service. And if someone asks me to consult the cards in an effort to find a missing person or to help solve a crime, I never accept any money. Each reader, of course, must decide for herself when, and under what conditions, she will accept money. Just remember where your talents originated and err on the side of spirituality and ethics. God will take care of the rest.

Let the cards "talk " to you. As you consider them, you will know exactly what to say if you listen to that inner voice. Do not question it. What the cards mean to YOU is what they mean. All minds do not think alike. An interesting note, even people who have never seen the cards before, often draw the same conclusions as those with years of experience! What better proof that the Tarot is an oracle?

Read your cards, respect them and enjoy them. As a hobby or as a vocation, reading the cards can be extremely fulfilling. There are many myths surrounding the cards. "You have to receive them as a gift." Not true. Buy a deck of cards that appeals to you. "You have to sleep with them under your pillow." Why? That seems like a fairly uncomfortable way to get some sleep, not to mention hard on the cards! I store my cards in a pretty wooden box, wrapped in one of my grandmother's handkerchiefs. They seem to work just fine. I buy a new deck when mine begin to look overly worn and ragged. I give my used decks to people who are interested in learning to read the cards but can't afford them, or to those who would just like to have them. Even Tarot cards can be recycled!

A Few Last Thoughts

Your delivery must be totally empathetic. It is not your calling to tell querents of impending doom or to frighten people. If, for example, you see the Three of Swords in a reading, do not say, "You have heart disease." Rather, say "Your cards indicate the lead-ins to heart disease...perhaps you would do well to periodically have your blood pressure or cholesterol checked." Interestingly, 99% of the time the person responds "I do have high blood pressure!" You will amaze yourself. Just remember, do not diagnose...just lead.

Touchy Subjects

There are many subjects in the world today that are extremely volatile. When doing a reading, you will often be asked questions that may reflect unfavorably on other people. Is my spouse cheating on me? Is my child in danger of being kidnapped by a non-custodial parent? Has my brother molested my child or his child? Did my son steal the $500.00 out of my purse?

These are very difficult situations to talk about. I recommend gently leading away from those subjects. If a parent really is concerned that her child has been molested or is in danger, a card reader is not the appropriate person with whom to discuss the problem. As a reader you have an obligation to be wise and fair, and it is neither wise nor fair to implicate someone in a heinous act. That is strictly a matter for the police. On the other hand, for example, if a child has already been kidnapped by a non-custodial parent, you are perfectly free to read what outcome is likely for that situation. Don't get caught up in accusations because that is not your place or calling. Steer people toward the appropriate professionals if the questions are too touchy. Realize that you have a great deal of power as a reader. What you say will be held in high esteem. You must exercise good judgement in what you say to people and about people.

TIPS FOR THE CLIENT

Tips for the querent

If you are looking for a reader, it is imperative to find one that is recommended by a friend. Preferably this should be a friend who is a long-time client of the reader. I wouldn't go looking in the personal ads for an otherwise unknown entity. If a reader is good, her reputation will be such that she will never have to advertise. And she wouldn't even dream of doing such a thing. Her clients come by word of mouth.

There are many unscrupulous people in the world, and for years card readers have been given a bad name. There are charlatans in every occupation, and card reading is no exception. A good reader will not frighten you. She will not ask you to purchase amulets, charms or candles. She will not promise magic to solve your problems. A good reader will listen to your questions and answer them as accurately as the cards allow. She will not add stipulations to her readings such as, "I'll be able to read you better if you buy me a piece of jewelry". You should feel comfortable with your reader. As you get to know one another, you will develop a bond.

Choose your reader as you would choose a friend. A friend would never ask you to go to any great lengths for her in return for listening to your concerns. Nor will a good reader. She will listen, interpret the cards for you, inform you of the options the cards dictate and offer you hope. And that is all it should be. She will not encourage you to come back week after week. If she is truthful, she will advise you to allow several months to pass so that the universe will have time to spin. If she is encouraging daily or weekly readings, and accepting money for them, look for another reader.

A good reader will offer you a private, quiet place for your reading. You should not be exposed to anyone else, unless you choose to have someone accompany you. If you wish to tape the session, you should be permitted to do so. It is your reading, and that is your choice. If a reader tells you that you must not reveal your reading to anyone, do not go back. That is an old trick used to control. Some readers who do this are telling the same thing to everyone, and they don't want you to begin comparing notes at the risk of being exposed as a fake.

You may tell anyone you wish about your reading. The reader, however, may not. Your reading is privileged information, and the rules of confidentiality apply. If you ever feel uncomfortable with a certain reader, or if she is predicting frightening things, acting strangely, or attempting to manipulate you, get up and walk out. You have that right. A card reading should be an enlightening experience that offers you hope. If there are problems in your life, a good reader will interpret the cards to give you your options regarding things you can do to help yourself.

Ideally, readers should be experienced at living so they have information to draw on. Older women seem to have the best knack for reading the cards; although, of course, anything is possible, and there may be a few wise 20-year-old readers out there! Again, keep an open mind when you have your reading.

Sometimes, it may seem that what the reader is predicting is impossible. Don't be too sure of that! Many times, what you think of as unlikely, will indeed transpire. As you begin to trust your reader, you will feel more confident in her predictions. If a reader you have been to many times expresses concern for your health, for example, make an appointment and get things checked out. At best, it will not be a problem. Yet if a reader is in tune with you, and she begins to know you, she is more likely to become medically intuitive about you. A good reader will not alarm you unnecessarily. Once a reader has established herself as fair and adept, you will hear many good things about her. That is the reader to choose.

ABOUT THE AUTHOR

Photograph by Tony Phung

Justine Alessi is a Master Tarot Reader and Teacher of the Tarot who brings over a decade of practical experience to the table. She has read the cards for people from almost every state in the Union, and word-of-mouth has people seeking her out for her wisdom and accuracy. Justine's uncanny accuracy makes believers out of the skeptical, and those who are initially the most hesitant are usually the first to try to acquire more of her time and talents. A former librarian, her interest in the Tarot was sparked by the parade of Tarot books published in the late 1980's. Feeling there was an inadequacy in the description of the cards, she began to compile her observations from years of readings. Justine is no stranger to writing, having penned many articles on the metaphysical and writing a newspaper column. Justine resides in Northeast Ohio with her husband, Robert and is the mother of two grown children. This is Justine's first book, though she is presently developing several more books regarding the Tarot, positive affirmation techniques and other metaphysical topics.

You may contact Ms. Alessi at www.justinealessi.com or by writing c/o: Ozark Mountain Publishing, Inc.
   PO Box 754
   Huntsville, AR 72740

ABOUT THE AUTHOR

M. E. McMillan brings life to the personalities in "Rebirth of the Oracle" by drawing on 20 years of creative writing experience. Ever prolific, Betsy works as a biomedical writer by day and spends her evenings and weekends (and sometimes her lunch hours) working on other creative writing projects. She is the author of two other books currently in print and does free-lance contract writing encompassing everything from bioscience to advertising copy. She is an active member of the National Writer's Union, and has appeared as a guest on several radio talk shows in Cleveland, Virginia, Texas, Michigan and Florida. Betsy resides in Northeast Ohio with her husband Jim and is the mother of two grown children. Presently she has several novels and non-fiction manuscripts in various stages of completion.

You may contact Ms. McMillan at www.memcmillan.com or by writing c/o: Ozark Mountain Publishing, Inc.
                                PO Box 754
                                Huntsville, AR 72740

Other Books by Ozark Mountain Publishing, Inc.

Dolores Cannon
A Soul Remembers Hiroshima
Between Death and Life
Conversations with Nostradamus,
    Volume I, II, III
The Convoluted Universe -Book One,
    Two, Three, Four, Five
The Custodians
Five Lives Remembered
Jesus and the Essenes
Keepers of the Garden
Legacy from the Stars
The Legend of Starcrash
The Search for Hidden Sacred Knowledge
They Walked with Jesus
The Three Waves of Volunteers and the
    New Earth
Aron Abrahamsen
Holiday in Heaven
Out of the Archives – Earth Changes
James Adams
Little Steps
Justine Alessi & M. E. McMillan
Rebirth of the Oracle
Kathryn/Patrick Andries
Naked in Public
Kathryn Andries
The Big Desire
Dream Doctor
Soul Choices: Six Paths to Find Your Life
    Purpose
Soul Choices: Six Paths to Fulfilling
    Relationships
Patrick Andries
Owners Manual for the Mind
Cat Baldwin
Divine Gifts of Healing
Dan Bird
Finding Your Way in the Spiritual Age
Waking Up in the Spiritual Age
Julia Cannon
Soul Speak – The Language of Your Body
Ronald Chapman
Seeing True
Albert Cheung
The Emperor's Stargate
Jack Churchward
Lifting the Veil on the Lost Continent of
    Mu
The Stone Tablets of Mu

Sherri Cortland
Guide Group Fridays
Raising Our Vibrations for the New Age
Spiritual Tool Box
Windows of Opportunity
Patrick De Haan
The Alien Handbook
Paulinne Delcour-Min
Holy Ice
Spiritual Gold
Anthony DeNino
The Power of Giving & Gratitude
Michael Dennis
Morning Coffee with God
God's Many Mansions
Carolyn Greer Daly
Opening to Fullness of Spirit
Anita Holmes
Twidders
Aaron Hoopes
Reconnecting to the Earth
Victoria Hunt
Kiss the Wind
Patricia Irvine
In Light and In Shade
Kevin Killen
Ghosts and Me
Diane Lewis
From Psychic to Soul
Donna Lynn
From Fear to Love
Maureen McGill
Baby It's You
Maureen McGill & Nola Davis
Live from the Other Side
Curt Melliger
Heaven Here on Earth
Henry Michaelson
And Jesus Said – A Conversation
Dennis Milner
Kosmos
Andy Myers
Not Your Average Angel Book
Guy Needler
Avoiding Karma
Beyond the Source – Book 1, Book 2
The Anne Dialogues
The Curators
The History of God
The Origin Speaks

For more information about any of the above titles, soon to be released titles,
or other items in our catalog, write, phone or visit our website:
PO Box 754, Huntsville, AR 72740
479-738-2348/800-935-0045
www.ozarkmt.com

Other Books by Ozark Mountain Publishing, Inc.

James Nussbaumer
And Then I Knew My Abundance
The Master of Everything
Mastering Your Own Spiritual Freedom
Sherry O'Brian
Peaks and Valleys
Riet Okken
The Liberating Power of Emotions
Gabrielle Orr
Akashic Records: One True Love
Let Miracles Happen
Victor Parachin
Sit a Bit
Nikki Pattillo
A Spiritual Evolution
Children of the Stars
Rev. Grant H. Pealer
A Funny Thing Happened on the
    Way to Heaven
Worlds Beyond Death
Victoria Pendragon
Born Healers
Feng Shui from the Inside, Out
Sleep Magic
The Sleeping Phoenix
Michael Perlin
Fantastic Adventures in Metaphysics
Walter Pullen
Evolution of the Spirit
Debra Rayburn
Let's Get Natural with Herbs
Charmian Redwood
A New Earth Rising
Coming Home to Lemuria
David Rivinus
Always Dreaming
Richard Rowe
Imagining the Unimaginable
M. Don Schorn
Elder Gods of Antiquity
Legacy of the Elder Gods
Gardens of the Elder Gods
Reincarnation...Stepping Stones of Life
Garnet Schulhauser
Dance of Eternal Rapture
Dance of Heavenly Bliss
Dancing Forever with Spirit

Dancing on a Stamp
Manuella Stoerzer
Headless Chicken
Annie Stillwater Gray
Education of a Guardian Angel
The Dawn Book
Joys of a Guardian Angel
Work of a Guardian Angel
Blair Styra
Don't Change the Channel
Who Catharted
Natalie Sudman
Application of Impossible Things
L.R. Sumpter
Judy's Story
The Old is New
We Are the Creators
Artur Tadevlsyan
Croton
Jim Thomas
Tales from the Trance
Jason & Jolene Tierney
A Quest of Transcendence
Nicholas Vesey
Living the Life-Force
Janie Wells
Embracing the Human Journey
Payment for Passage
Dennis Wheatley/ Maria Wheatley
The Essential Dowsing Guide
Maria Wheatley
Druidic Soul Star Astrology
Jacquelyn Wiersma
The Zodiac Recipe
Sherry Wilde
The Forgotten Promise
Lyn Willmoth
A Small Book of Comfort
Stuart Wilson & Joanna Prentis
Atlantis and the New Consciousness
Beyond Limitations
The Essenes -Children of the Light
The Magdalene Version
Power of the Magdalene
Robert Winterhalter
The Healing Christ

For more information about any of the above titles, soon to be released titles,
or other items in our catalog, write, phone or visit our website:
PO Box 754, Huntsville, AR 72740
479-738-2348/800-935-0045
www.ozarkmt.com

CPSIA information can be obtained
at www.ICGtesting.com
Printed in the USA
BVHW040223261120
594271BV00030B/564

9 781886 940895